THE UNIVERSITY OF MICHIGAN
CENTER FOR CHINESE STUDIES

MICHIGAN PAPERS IN CHINESE STUDIES
NO. 22

BETWEEN TWO PLENUMS:
CHINA'S INTRALEADERSHIP CONFLICT,
1959-1962

by
Ellis Joffe

Ann Arbor

Center for Chinese Studies
The University of Michigan

1975

Open access edition funded by the National Endowment for the Humanities/ Andrew W. Mellon Foundation Humanities Open Book Program.

Printed and bound by CPI Group (UK) Ltd, Croydon, CR0 4YY

ISBN 978-0-89264-022-5 (hardcover)
ISBN 978-0-472-03836-7 (paper)
ISBN 978-0-472-12813-6 (ebook)
ISBN 978-0-472-90213-2 (open access)

CONTENTS

ACKNOWLEDGMENTS

The major part of this short monograph was completed while I was a Research Associate at The University of Michigan's Center for Chinese Studies during the academic year 1971-72. For enabling me to spend this year at Michigan, from which I derived immense personal pleasure and professional benefit, and for the hospitality accorded me, I am deeply grateful to the directors and members of the Center for Chinese Studies. I am especially indebted to Professors Albert Feuerwerker, Rhoads Murphey, Michel Oksenberg, Allen Whiting, Ernest Young and Dr. David Denny for commenting on the manuscript, to Professor Oksenberg for taking the trouble to write a preface, to Jeannie Lin for editing the text, and to Ros Daly for many favors. I alone, of course, am responsible for the final product.

Ellis Joffe
The Hebrew University
of Jerusalem
May 1975

FOREWORD

Quebec, Cairo, Teheran, Yalta, Potsdam . . . mention of
these dramatic World War II diplomatic conferences immediately
sparks debates among American diplomatic historians who have
different reconstructions of these turning points in world history.

Thanks particularly to documentation obtained during the Cultural Revolution, Western analysts of contemporary China now proudly
possess a similar roll call of meetings to hash and rehash: for example from the the late 1958-62 era, Wuhan, 1958; Second Chengchow;
Lushan, 1959; the Ninth Plenum; the Grandview Guest House meeting;
the Meeting of the 7000; the West Guest House meeting; and the Tenth
Plenum. To the nonspecialist outsider, these names may seem esoteric, mysterious. But to the leaders of China, the list immediately
evokes vivid memories of crucial meetings where they grappled with
problems of the immediate post-Great Leap era: the economic de-
pression; the growing Sino-Soviet dispute; and the nation's loss of
ideological commitment.

Students of post-1949 Chinese politics generally agree that the
1959-62 era was pivotal, and that the fate of the nation hung in the
balance at the meetings which Ellis Joffe seeks to untangle in this
useful monograph. Scholars also tend to believe that the elite tensions which culminated in the Cultural Revolution of 1966-69 arose
at least as early as 1959-62. However, little agreement exists over
precisely what happened during those years or how it happened. In
particular, many argue that Mao Tse-tung slipped from power in those
years and that Liu Shao-ch'i led the post-Leap economic and political
rehabilitation, largely in opposition to Mao. According to this argument, the Cultural Revolution was Mao's way of regaining power lost
initially in 1958-62.

The research for this monograph was done in 1971-72 in Ann
Arbor when Professor Joffe was a Research Associate of the Center
for Chinese Studies, but the writing was completed in Israel in 1973-
74. Rejecting a "Mao-in-command" model, he highlights elite strife,
and argues that the 1958-62 era involved a complex interplay among
the top leaders. Through his reading of the Cultural Revolution materials released through 1972, Joffe concludes that after Lushan, Mao's

ix

x

personal power was challenged at the major Party meetings. Joffe
believes that Mao was able to publically maintain an image of consensus among his associates throughout the difficult period through
ambiguity and obfuscating of controversial issues. But Mao was not
always successful, and on several occasions the lines of conflict were
sharply drawn.

A word on Joffe's sources is appropriate. He draws extensively
upon the so-called "Cultural Revolution" or "Red Guard" materials,
e.g., publications of various nongovernmental groups during the
1966-69 era. The pamphlets, newspapers, posters, and handbills
were based in part on materials secured through raids on state and
Party archives and through official leaks. These materials then fil-
tered out of China to Hong Kong and elsewhere, where they were
procured by various research agencies. Since the information in
these materials is not always reliable--for example, Red Guard
charges against Liu Shao-ch'i or Teng Hsiao-p'ing seem distorted--
care is required in using them.

Ellis Joffe has sought confirmation of Red Guard accusations
through the documentation of the time. For example, he substan-
tiates some Red Guard revelations about the 1959 Lushan Plenum
through a careful reading of People's Daily of 1959 and through 1959-
60 reports of informed Western observers. Further, Joffe has tried
to draw primarily upon Red Guard reproductions of entire speeches;
by and large, he admits that short quotations could easily have been
taken out of context. Finally, he has not accepted Red Guard por-
trayals of the motivations, personalities, and personal relations of
various Chinese leaders; instead, he has focused upon Red Guard
disclosures of actual words and deeds.

As a result, Joffe's reconstruction of 1959-62 differs in instances
from the picture proposed by the Red Guards and by Western analysts
who have perhaps overexuberantly accepted Red Guard charges. The
net effect is that Joffe argues that a cleavage between Mao and his
associates erupted during the 1959-62 era, but the fissure between
the two lines was not as sharply drawn as it was to become in 1965-
66. It is a valuable and timely argument to have in print.

Michel Oksenberg
Ann Arbor, Michigan
March 1975

INTRODUCTION

Since the Cultural Revolution erupted on the Chinese political scene, more seems to have been written about this great upheaval than about its origins. Two main reasons probably account for this. First, the Cultural Revolution was an epic political struggle unprecedented in its dimensions and openness in the history of the regime; accordingly, it is bound to be more rewarding to researchers than the opaque political maneuverings which preceded it. More importantly, because the Cultural Revolution was a relatively open affair, it threw up reams of materials which, for all their shortcomings, enable the analyst to follow the development of the upheaval in a more direct fashion than any other episode in the annals of the Chinese People's Republic. To be sure, these materials also constitute a major source for the study of the pre-Cultural Revolution period, but they are much less revealing and reliable about this period than about the Cultural Revolution itself. Thus, it is easier to trace the course of the Cultural Revolution than to delve into the conflicts and controversies which caused it.

The difficulty of dealing with the pre-Cultural Revolution period is underlined by the fact that scholars who have studied this period are divided in their interpretations. These scholars can be grouped, perhaps somewhat simplistically, into two basically divergent schools of thought. According to Frederick Teiwes,* the first school exhibits "a widespread tendency . . . to adopt, albeit with significant variations and modifications, concepts derived from Peking's own 'two line struggle' . . . model of political conflict." Teiwes characterizes this school as follows:

> The central assumption shared by proponents of this view
> is that Chinese politics was long marked by tension be-
> tween two antithetical approaches. One, identified with
> Mao, sought modernization through mass mobilization
> and manifested a deep concern with the ideological purity
> of Chinese society. The opposing approach, ascribed to
> the grey Party bureaucracy and personified and led by

* Frederick C. Teiwes, "Chinese Politics 1949-1965: A Changing Mao." Current Scene, January 1974, vol. XII, no. 1, pp. 1-15; and February 1974, vol. XII, no. 2, pp. 1-19.

1

Liu Shao-ch'i, was absorbed in the prosaic tasks of
production and economic growth, wedded to rational
strategies in dealing with China's problems, and ob-
sessed with orderly development of the existing system. . . . Fluctuations in Party policies are seen
in terms of significant and often bitter conflict between advocates of each position in which the political
balance has often been delicate, with Mao sometimes
suffering losses of power.

Teiwes, as well as other scholars who share his approach
to one degree of another, reject this interpretation. Teiwes ob-
jects to several basic assumptions of the "conflict" school, namely,
that the Chinese leadership tended to polarize around dichotomous
positions, that shifts in policies primarily reflected the continuing
conflict among the leaders, and that this conflict brought about
significant variations in Mao's power. While conceding that leadership differences figured in fluctuating Party policies prior to the
Cultural Revolution, Teiwes maintains that "Mao himself has fre-
quently changed his position both in terms of specific policies and
by emphasizing different aspects of his intellectual outlook." Teiwes
ascribes these changes of direction either to Mao's dialectical view
of the world as gripped in a state of constant flux or, on a more
concrete level, to the dynamic tension between a series of contradictory policy approaches, with first one than another in ascendancy.
Teiwes concludes, therefore, that "divergent tendencies in Mao's
thought, whether due to Mao's rigorous analysis of a given situation,
his personal preoccupations of the moment or the efforts of others
to apply his thought to problems at hand go a long way in explaining
shifting CCP policies."

Thus, as against the "two line struggle" interpretation of the
first school, the second school puts forth a "Mao in command" expla-
nation of pre-Cultural Revolution Chinese politics. While the first
school maintains that the widely held pre-1965 "consensus" view of
Chinese leadership politics was demolished by the disclosures of the
Cultural Revolution, and, indeed, by the Cultural Revolution itself,
the second school continues to subscribe to this view. According to
its interpretation, throughout the period leading up to the Cultural
Revolution Mao's position within the leadership was predominant and
there was no serious disagreement with Mao's concepts. In this situation, there were no grounds for the emergence of two basically
opposing policy lines. When sharp shifts in policy did occur, they

occurred not because Mao's opponents gained the upper hand, but because Mao himself experienced a change of heart.

The origins of the Cultural Revolution, in short, are still shrouded in uncertainty. Crucial questions either remain unanswered or have been given answers which derive from conflicting interpretations. To what period can the direct origins of the Cultural Revolution be traced? What issues, if any, divided the leadership, and how deep were these divisions? What was the state of power relations and what was Mao's position? Why did developments in the period preceding the Cultural Revolution reach a climax in such a convulsion? These are some of the questions which have to be investigated in order to understand the origins of the Cultural Revolution.

The purpose of this short monograph, which is meant to be part of a larger study, is to examine these questions as they applied to the years 1959-1962. More specifically, it deals with the period between two Plenums of the CCP's Central Committee, the Eighth Plenum, held in August 1959, and the Tenth Plenum, held in September 1962. Its approach leans heavily toward the first interpretation, although it takes into account salient and significant points made by scholars of the second school. Basically, then, this monograph subscribes to the "conflict" rather than the "consensus" view of pre-Cultural Revolution politics. From this vantage point, the Eighth and Tenth Plenums loom in retrospect as important watersheds in the development of the intraleadership conflict which culminated in the great upheaval. The years bracketed by these Plenums constitute the formative stage of this conflict. This stage began with the Eighth Plenum, when the basic rift among the top leaders first came to the fore, and ended with the Tenth Plenum, after which this rift was played out primarily in the form of subterranean struggles, which broke through the surface in the explosion of 1966.

The monograph makes no attempt to survey the entire spectrum of developments during this stage of the intraleadership conflict, nor to provide all the available details of the events which are surveyed. Its limited purpose is to single out those threads which stretch directly to the Cultural Revolution in order to shed some light on the origins of this most dramatic chapter in the post-1949 history of the regime.

The Great Leap Forward

The first question confronting the analyst attempting to trace the origins of the Cultural Revolution is how far back these origins lie. Should they be sought in the early years of the regime, when cleavages between the top leaders, primarily Mao Tse-tung and Liu Shao-ch'i, were already apparent? Or should they be sought even before the establishment of the regime, in the different revolutionary experience and orientation of the Chinese leaders?[1] If so, can the Cultural Revolution be viewed merely as the climax of a conflict that had been gathering momentum throughout the years? The answer, as best as can be determined, is in the negative. For while intra-leadership differences existed before and after the establishment of the regime, until the Great Leap Forward of 1958-1959 these differences were contained within a broader framework of unity and cohesion. It was only when the Great Leap Forward began to collapse that this unity started to disintegrate. For this collapse released a multitude of currents which swirled on the Chinese political scene with gathering force in the subsequent years until they finally converged in the tidal wave of the Cultural Revolution. The magnitude of the repercussions triggered by the collapse of the Great Leap Forward can be appreciated only in the light of the Great Leap's overwhelming significance in the short history of the regime.[2]

Until the Cultural Revolution, the Great Leap Forward was the great watershed in China's national development: it marked the final abandonment of the Soviet-oriented model of industralization, and the adoption of a bold new approach. Dramatic in principle and daring in practice, this approach constituted the Chinese way to modernization. It emerged from a search which got underway roughly in 1955, when many Chinese leaders started to express guarded but growing doubts about the suitability of Soviet methods of development to China.[3]

These doubts, in large part, related to China's economic performance, and were generated by the fact that although the first five-year plan, which had been patterned on the Soviet example, had re-

4

sulted in highly impressive advances in the industrial sector, agricultural production had failed to keep pace. And the Chinese leadership was acutely aware that the momentum of industrial growth could not be sustained unless the agricultural surplus was greatly increased. One possible way to overcome this problem was to divert resources from industry to agriculture, but this alternative was obviously unacceptable to a leadership bent on rapid industrialization. The other alternative, deriving from the Soviet example, was to extract a much greater surplus from the countryside without investing more resources in it. This alternative, however, was also unacceptable, partly because rural living standards were already extremely low, and partly because the Chinese leadership, unlike Stalin, had a unique relationship with the peasantry and was unwilling to subject it to more hardships.[4] What the Chinese leadership had to find, therefore, was a way to increase the agricultural surplus by increasing production without large material investments in the rural areas. Its solution, hammered out after debates, was to achieve this increase primarily through the institutional means of collectivization, which, in contrast with the Soviet Union, was intended mainly to raise agricultural output rather than to increase extractions through greater regimentation.[5] Collectivization, however, failed to provide the agricultural surplus required by the ambitious industrial goals, and this realization set the Chinese leaders off on the search for a way out of the dilemma. This search led them to the Great Leap Forward.

Adding impetus and urgency to this search was the mounting concern of some Chinese leaders, most notably Mao, over the sociopolitical consequences of importing Soviet methods of development. Although the Chinese had preserved some of their unique revolutionary techniques even as they transplanted the essentials of the Soviet model, they began to perceive that, on balance, this transplantation was spawning offshoots which were sharply at variance with their revolutionary experience and postrevolutionary expectations. For it was clear that under Soviet influence the Chinese revolution was becoming routinized, and that China's revolutionaries were becoming bureaucratized. Mao, as well as other leaders committed to Mao's social vision, were not prepared to accept methods of development which led to these consequences.[6]

Thus, by the mid-1950s two major trends of thinking seemed to converge within the Chinese leadership. Although these trends stemmed from different perceptions, cumulatively they highlighted the shortcomings of the Soviet model. Some leaders probably saw these shortcomings primarily in terms of China's economic development. Others, like Mao, were no less concerned with the socio-political ramifications of the Soviet model. The disillusionment with the Soviet model, in short, derived from a combination of reasons, but whatever the reasons of individual leaders, the result seemed to be a broad consensus at the apex of the Chinese hierarchy on the need to strike out in new directions.

As they groped for a new strategy of development, the Chinese leaders began to turn more and more to their own revolutionary experience as a source of guidance and inspiration. In the process, the mass-oriented elements of Mao's revolutionary ideology, which had been submerged during the heyday of Soviet influence, began to surface with increasing intensity and to acquire new dimensions. Looking at their current problems through the prism of their past experience, the Chinese leaders came to the conclusion that the methods which had brought them success in the revolutionary period could also be applied to the present. The wellspring of these methods was their belief in the ability of the "human element"--properly motivated and properly mobilized masses--to overcome seemingly insuperable material obstacles. And it was this belief, transferred from the struggle for power to the struggle for development, that became the motive force behind the Great Leap Forward. [7]

The primary objective of the Great Leap was to achieve an economic breakthrough by the rapid and simultaneous development of both industry and agriculture through the maximum utilization of China's labor force in mass movements. In this way, by "walking on two legs," the leadership sought to sustain the rapid pace of industrial growth and, at the same time, to increase the agricultural output. The assumption underlying this great national effort was that the vast masses of the Chinese people--China's most precious asset--constitute a tremendous storehouse of productive energy which, if released, could move mountains through sheer human will power. In order to release and channel this energy, the regime relied on the maximum mobilization of the masses for supreme efforts on labor-intensive projects through a combination of ideological exhortation and Party leadership at the grass-roots level. [8]

Although the goals of the Great Leap Forward were stated primarily in economic terms, its underlying concepts and methods had important socio-political implications. Such prominent features of the Great Leap as mass participation, the shift of power from "experts" to "reds," the attempt to narrow the gap between city and countryside, and the stress on egalitarianism--these and other features had the combined effect of stemming the trend toward bureaucratization and social stratification which had characterized Chinese society during the years of Soviet influence. To some of China's revolutionary leaders, in short, the Great Leap had an appeal that went far beyond its economic context. [9]

The Great Leap Forward thus appears to have meant different things to different leaders. To those leaders whose primary aim was swift economic development, and whose dissatisfaction with the Soviet model had stemmed mainly from its economic inadequacies, the strategy of the Great Leap probably appeared to be the most sensible way to achieve this aim. To others, who had been concerned about the social implications of the Soviet model, the Great Leap not only held out the prospect of rapid development, but also promised to infuse new life into the Chinese revolution. Thus, while individual leaders probably attached varying degrees of importance to the different components of the Great Leap, their goals seemed to converge in the new strategy of development. And it was this convergence that presumably welded the general consensus which was apparently reached among China's top leaders as the new strategy was worked out. [10]

In retrospect, however, it is clear that this consensus implicitly rested on a fragile foundation. For in order to preserve it, the Great Leap had to fulfill the diverse expectations of a wide range of leaders. When the whole effort collapsed and many of these expectations lay shattered in its ruins, the leadership consensus broke down. This breakdown set off the disputes which formed the major theme of intra-Party relations in the first half of the 1960s, and which linked the collapse of the Great Leap with the Cultural Revolution.

For several months after the Great Leap got underway in earnest in the spring of 1958, it appeared as if the utopian visions of the Chinese leadership were turning into reality. The entire nation seemed to be gripped by a spirit of determination and dedication which seemingly moved it to achieve miraculous results. Hard-driving local cadres, caught in the euphoric mood radiated by the central leadership, spurred the masses to a feverish pitch of endeavor. On their part, the masses, responding to the exhortations and pressures of the leadership, appeared to turn China into a veritable beehive of activity. Communes were set up to facilitate the mobilization of China's man-

power, and to bring the country closer to Mao's social vision.
"Backyard steel furnaces" were promoted throughout the nation to
aid the industrial effort.   Unrealistic production targets were set,
and then, on the basis of exaggerated reports, were further raised.[11]

It did not take the Chinese leadership long to realize that the
gigantic effort was getting out of hand, and that its excesses were
leading the nation along a dangerous road.   At a series of meetings
convened while the Great Leap was in progress, the leadership mod-
erated some of these excesses, but no attempt was made to halt the
campaign.[12]   At one of these meetings, the Wuhan conference of
December 1958, Mao relinquished his ceremonial post of Chairman
of the Republic.   If this move on Mao's part was, in contrast with
what the Chinese claimed, not entirely voluntary, then it appears
that the difficulties generated by the Great Leap Forward already
began to disrupt leadership relations.[13]   Be that as it may, the
great explosion at the pinnacle of the Chinese power pyramid was
yet to come.

The Eighth Plenum and The P'eng Teh-huai Affair

This explosion occurred at the Lushan conference held in July-
August 1959, which began with a series of meetings and ended with
a full-scale plenum of the Central Committee.   By this time it had
become apparent to the Chinese leadership that it had fallen victim
to its grandiose hopes, and now had to come to grips with the consequences.   And the consequences were ominous.   The Great Leap
Forward was faltering.   Its excesses had caused widespread and
severe dislocations.   A major crisis was clearly looming on the
Chinese economic horizon.[14]

In the shadow of this gathering storm, the Chinese leaders met
to reappraise their policies.   But what was intended as a policy reappraisal quickly turned into a power struggle at the top level of the
ruling hierarchy, pitting Mao against several leading figures, and
precipitating the gravest leadership crisis since the Communists came
to power.[15]   This crisis erupted when Marshal P'eng Teh-huai, then
Minister of Defense and a member of the Politburo, supported by
several important leaders, launched an assault on the policies of the
Great Leap Forward, an assault which Mao regarded as a challenge
to his personal leadership, and to which he responded accordingly.

Although some six years were to elapse between the Lushan Affair and the start of the Cultural Revolution, from the perspective of hindsight it is possible to discern several strands which stretched from this affair to the Cultural Revolution.

For one thing, P'eng himself was to become, although largely in a passive fashion, a key figure in the shadowy struggle that began to shape up at the highest levels of the Chinese power structure in the early 1960s. For another, although P'eng and his associates were denounced at Lushan and dismissed from their posts, the views which P'eng expressed were evidently shared, if not articulated at Lushan, by many members of the ruling group. As the crisis which P'eng had predicted materialized with dramatic intensity, these views surfaced and became a major source of the leadership conflict which led to the Cultural Revolution. In a broader context, what distinguished the P'eng Teh-huai Affair from earlier disputes within the Chinese leadership was the linkage of policy issues with power relations and questions of leadership involving Mao himself; and it was this linkage, greatly magnified, which formed the major theme underlying the process that propelled the Chinese leadership to the Cultural Revolution.

The immediate spark that ignited the struggle at Lushan was P'eng Teh-huai's so-called "Letter of Opinion," which he sent to Mao on July 14, and also distributed to his colleagues at the conference.[16] In this document P'eng set forth his views on the economic consequences of the Great Leap. Although he obviously tried to maintain an even-handed approach, there can be little doubt that these views amounted to a bitter indictment of the Great Leap Forward, which, in P'eng's opinion, brought much more damage than benefits. And it was this damage, as P'eng himself admitted when interrogated by the Red Guards several years later, that he had highlighted in his letter. "There were both losses and gains in the Great Leap Forward of 1958," P'eng said, "but the losses were predominant."[17]

Nonetheless, P'eng made a point of also stressing the achievements. These, he said, were "affirmed and undoubted," and were especially important "in a country like ours where the economic foundation is weak and technical equipment is backward." However, some capital construction projects were "too hasty or excessive," and as a result "imbalances and . . . temporary difficulties were created."[18]

The formation of the rural communes, P'eng went on, was of "great significance." Although there had been "a period of confusion regarding the questions of the system of ownership and some shortcomings and errors appeared," P'eng conceded that the "chaotic condition is basically over."[19] Whether P'eng really thought so or merely considered it prudent to tone down his criticism of the communes is a moot point, because shortly before writing his letter P'eng had spoken at meetings convened in preparation for the Plenum, and had been much more outspoken on the communes. The communes, he argued, had been "set up too soon. The superiority of the higher cooperatives had just manifested itself, but had not developed to the full extent. Furthermore, the switchover to the people's communes had not been tested. Had we experimented with it for a year, everything would be well."[20]

The "backyard steel furnace" campaign, in P'eng's view, was also a product of rashness. Small blast furnaces, he said in his letter, were needlessly built; as a result material and human resources had been wasted.[21]

The experience of the Great Leap Forward, P'eng continued, had yielded "a good number of profound lessons," and in drawing these lessons his criticism became much more caustic. For one thing, he implicitly condemned the whole Maoist concept of permanent revolution. "We have," he said, "not understood sufficiently the socialist laws of planned and proportionate development." For another, he claimed that the Great Leap resulted in shortages, and these shortages strained the regime's relations with the population. The people, P'eng warned, demand a change.[22]

The difficulties, in P'eng's view, stemmed from two principal defects in the work style of the Party. First, there was "the habit of exaggeration," as a result of which "unbelievable miracles" were reported, and "tremendous harm" was done to the prestige of the Party. Due to the exaggerations, "extravagance and waste" became widespread--"we considered ourselves rich while actually we were still poor."[23]

Secondly, the Party had become afflicted with "petty-bourgeois fanaticism," which caused it to commit "leftist" mistakes. In its haste to enter the era of communism, the Party forgot "the style of seeking truth from facts," failed to take account of "concrete conditions," and neglected "scientific and economic laws."[24]

The roots of these defects, P'eng implied, lay in the Maoist approach that "putting politics in command could be a substitute for everything." P'eng rejected such an approach. "Putting politics in command," he said, "is no substitute for economic principles, still less for the concrete measures in economic work. Equal importance must be attached to politics in command and the effective measures in economic work; neither can be overestimated or neglected."[25]

Despite his criticism, P'eng clearly made an attempt to disassociate Mao himself from the policies which he was denouncing. P'eng began his critique on a humble and self-effacing note: "I write this letter to you for reference . . . I am a simple man . . . and have no tact . . . If what I say is wrong, please correct me." P'eng then went out of his way to pin responsibility for excesses of the Great Leap not on Mao's policies, but on the faulty understanding of these policies by the leading officials:

> Although the Chairman had last year called on the whole
> Party to combine sky-rocketing zeal with scientific anal-
> ysis and set forth the policy of walking on two legs, it
> appears that both the call and the policy had not been
> appreciated by the majority of leading comrades. I am
> of course no exception.[26]

The purpose of his letter, P'eng emphasized, was to increase understanding, and not to apportion blame. "On the whole," he said, "there should be no investigation of personal responsibility."[27]

From the critique it seems clear, therefore, that P'eng had no intention of challenging the personal leadership of Mao, let alone of unseating the Chairman. There was no conceivable reason for P'eng to contemplate such an extreme step, nor any reason for him to assume that he could muster sufficient support to challenge Mao personally, even in the extremely unlikely case that this was his objective. What then was P'eng's objective? Although this is not clear from the published documents, on balance it seems reasonable to assume that P'eng and his associates set themselves the limited objective of persuading, and probably pressuring, Mao to moderate the extreme policies of the Great Leap Forward and to bring about a basic shift in policy. As P'eng said in his letter: ". . . While drawing up plans for next year (1960) we should all the more seriously consider them on the basis of seeking truth from facts and on a reliable foundation."[28]

If Mao's position had been weakened at the Wuhan conference because of the difficulties caused by the Great Leap, P'eng may have assumed that the intensification of these difficulties since the conference would strengthen the hand of those leaders who wanted a change.[29] But even leaving the Wuhan conference aside, P'eng probably figured that the already apparent shortcomings of the Great Leap would persuade a sufficient number of his colleagues to back him in his effort to bring about a policy shift.

Behind P'eng's determination to effect such a shift, there were presumably a number of motives, stemming from his dual role as a member of China's top policy-making group and as chief of China's armed forces. These motives were related both to the immediate consequences of the Great Leap, and to its broader implications. In the first place, P'eng was doubtless deeply distressed by the suffering which, in his view, would be inflicted upon the peasantry by the excesses of the Great Leap, and on this score alone he could, in his words, "remain reticent no more."[30] Second, his concern for the plight of the peasantry was probably reinforced by the apprehension, which turned out to be justified, that the hardships in the countryside would severely affect the morale of the troops.[31] Third, the policies of the Great Leap Forward required the heavy involvement of the army in economic and other nonmilitary activities, which disrupted its regular programs and caused dissent in the professional officer corps.[32]

But whereas P'eng was undoubtedly perturbed by these consequences of the Great Leap, it seems strange that it was he who took the initiative in voicing a critique based on economic considerations. For although P'eng was a member of the top ruling group, his main area of concern was national defense, and there is no indication that in the past he had shown any special interest in economic policies. Why then was it P'eng, rather than leaders who dealt specifically with economic matters, who spoke out at Lushan? Perhaps P'eng's sensitivity to the fate of the peasantry and his outspoken nature may form part of the answer. But only a small part at most. For, as best as can be determined, the economic policy of the Great Leap Forward was only one of several interrelated issues which converged in the conflict at Lushan. And it was precisely these other issues which affected P'eng directly as head of China's military establishment, and which for him, more than for leaders concerned with other areas of national policy, made a showdown urgent. These issues encompassed, to one degree or another, the whole range of national defense: strategic policy, Sino-Soviet military relations, and the future development of the military establishment.

The materials on the Lushan Plenum, which the Chinese released officially or which appeared in Red Guard publications, reveal almost nothing about the strategic and military issues at Lushan, presumably because of their sensitivity, and hence do not convey the significance of these issues in the conflict. However, on the basis of circumstantial and other evidence it is clear that these issues cast a giant shadow over the entire plenum, and figured prominently in the motives and moves of the participants in the drama. Although many important details are unknown, enough is known about these issues to attempt a brief assessment of their impact on the Lushan Plenum.

Such an assessment must be made against the background of the strategic-military problems which confronted, and divided, the Chinese leadership on the eve of the Lushan conference. Insofar as they were relevant to what was presumably discussed at the conference, these problems boiled down to one basic question: How should China develop a nuclear capability, and what military and strategic policies should the leadership adopt while China is moving toward the development of this capability? One school of thought, which centered in the professional officer corps, and for which P'eng Teh-huai was the chief spokesman, advocated reliance on Soviet aid for the development of China's nuclear program, and reliance on the Soviet nuclear shield in the international arena while this development was in progress. In the conventional field, these officers urged that the PLA continue to be developed along the Soviet model in the direction of a highly professional, modernized, and mechanized army, conditioned to fight a positional war in the defense of the mainland. From the vantage point of these officers, then, Soviet aid was crucial in three vital and interconnected areas: military strategy in international politics; nuclear development; and the progress of China's conventional forces. However, in the months preceding the Lushan conference, it had become increasingly clear to the Chinese that the price which the Soviets put on such aid was the acceptance by China of the Soviet line in international affairs, and, to some extent, in domestic policy as well. This was a price the Chinese officers were apparently prepared to pay, or at least to negotiate, for what they considered the overriding interest of national security. For this reason, they viewed the deterioration of Sino-Soviet relations with growing concern, a concern which must have reached a high point on the eve of the Lushan conference when, in June 1959, the Soviets abrogated a secret agreement on the sharing of nuclear technology which, according to the Chinese, had been concluded in October 1957. [33]

The views of P'eng Teh-huai and his associates in the professional officer corps were rejected by Mao and his supporters. For Mao was prepared to risk a rift with the Soviets, whatever the cost, if the condition of the Soviets for continuing the relationship was that the Chinese had to accept the position of a junior partner, and to toe the Soviet line in areas where Mao was convinced he was right and Khrushchev was wrong. If the price for what Mao regarded as the safeguarding of China's independence and integrity was the loss of Soviet aid, he was quite willing to pay it. In that case, however, reliance on the Soviets had to be replaced by "self-reliance." [34]

For the military establishment this stand had several far-reaching implications. The starting point was that China would have to develop its own nuclear capability on the basis of indigenous efforts, and all available resources would have to be allocated for the attainment of this goal. Since China's resources were limited, the concentration on the nuclear program meant that it would have to come at the expense of a further large-scale development of the conventional forces. And since the political decisions which led to the concentration on an indigenous nuclear program in the first place cast heavy doubt on the continued availability of even conventional equipment from the Soviets, and net effect of "self-reliance" was that, aside from select areas crucial to defense, the progress of China's conventional forces would, by and large, have to be frozen. Such a step was feasible, the Maoists contended, because by 1958 these forces had reached a level of development that was adequate for the defense of China (neither Mao nor the professional officers, it must be emphasized, argued in terms of an offensive war). The Maoist view, however, was based on the pivotal assumption that the PLA would be oriented to fight a war by relying primarily not on sophisticated weaponry and a conventional strategy, as it had been trained to do during the period of Soviet-oriented modernization, but by relying on the "human element" and the Maoist doctrine of a "people's war."

This was a strategy which many military and political leaders were willing to accept as a solution to China's quest for both political independence and military security. But although China's leadership seemed to be moving toward this solution at least from the summer of 1958, one major obstacle still remained in the way of its final adoption: the opposition of P'eng Teh-huai and his supporters in the professional officer corps. Thus, when P'eng launched his assault at Lushan, there was much more involved than the economic issues which he raised.[35]

Given the complexity of the issues and P'eng's stake in them, it may be asked why P'eng limited his attack only to the economic policies of the Great Leap Forward. To begin with, this question may be based on an erroneous assumption, since it is quite possible that P'eng spoke out on other issues as well, but the Maoists, for reasons of their own, chose to release only his economic critique. Without speculating on this, however, there seemed to have been sound reasons, apart from his already mentioned concern about the peasantry, for P'eng to focus his attack on the Great Leap Forward. These reasons probably stemmed from P'eng's effort to appeal simultaneously to two constituencies, his colleagues on the Central Committee as well as the Soviet leadership, in the hope that a shift in China's policies would, in turn, bring about a shift in Soviet policies toward China.

P'eng undoubtedly assumed that to influence his colleagues on the basis of military and strategic arguments would be an extremely difficult, if not impossible task. For the wind at the top level of China's leadership was blowing in the opposite direction, and policies which rejected the views of P'eng and his supporters were gaining ground. In these circumstances, P'eng could hardly have hoped to persuade his intensely nationalistic colleagues to accept what they regarded as an affront to China's national dignity on the grounds that this was necessary for the more important purpose of shoring up China's security. For to them, China's security, once they accepted the Maoist strategy, was in no urgent need of shoring up. There was, in short, a wide gap between the perspectives of P'eng Teh-huai and his nonmilitary colleagues, a gap that was rooted in their different areas of specialization, and the different organizational pressures which influenced them.

No such gap, however, existed with respect to economic policies. All the leaders were directly affected and deeply concerned about these policies, and their concern mounted as the Great Leap Forward began to crumble. P'eng may have thought, therefore, that whereas he could not muster support on military-strategic grounds, a critique of the Great Leap Forward and its economic effects would gain widespread acceptance. If this was P'eng's reasoning, he was, as will be seen, proven right. Where he went wrong was in his assumption that he could appeal both to his colleagues and to the Soviet leadership at the same time. And it was this mistake that played a major role in his downfall.

Assuming that P'eng's critique was intended to generate pressure for a shift in the policies of the Great Leap, what relevance did this have for Sino-Soviet military relations? For one thing, the Great Leap and, especially, the doctrinal claims which the Chinese made for it, constituted a major factor behind the deterioration of Sino-Soviet relations. For the Chinese triumphantly declared that the Great Leap Forward was moving China to the threshhold of Communism, which meant ahead of the Soviet Union. This oblique but unmistakable challenge to one facet of Soviet leadership of the Communist bloc infuriated the Soviets. [36] Perhaps P'eng thought that the moderation of China's internal policies and the deflation of their doctrinal implications would contribute to an improvement of Sino-Soviet relations. This, in turn, would make it possible for the Soviets to reconsider their nuclear aid, to say nothing of continuing their supply of conventional equipment. [37]

P'eng may have further assumed that, since the projected achievements of the Great Leap formed the basis of the leadership's hopes for "self-reliance," a shift to less ambitious policies necessitated by the failure of the Leap would convince his colleagues that going it alone in the economic field was impractical. What was more practical was to lay the foundations for China's economic and technological development by utilizing Soviet aid. And such aid could be forthcoming if the Chinese leadership made an effort to improve its relations with the Soviets. [38]

If these were some of P'eng's calculations, he was probably not operating in a vacuum. Having had close contacts with the Soviets over the years, and having visited Eastern Europe for almost two months shortly before the Lushan conference, a visit during which he had met with Khrushchev, it is possible that P'eng had been in some sort of communication with the Soviet leader regarding Chinese domestic politics and Sino-Soviet relations. [39] The nature of this communication is speculative at best. But one possibility is

that P'eng let Khrushchev know of his dissatisfaction with the policies of the Chinese leadership, and had reached some kind of understanding with the Soviet leader that if he succeeded in bringing about
a change in Chinese policies and posture, the Soviets would renew,
and perhaps expand, their nuclear aid program. In the light of this
conjecture the Maoist charge that P'eng "informed baldheaded Khrushchev of the shortcomings of the Great Leap Forward, and the latter
encouraged the former to go home and oppose Chairman Mao,"[40]
appears to have some substance. It need hardly be added that for
Khrushchev, any move that would weaken the Maoist group and
strengthen elements in the Chinese leadership with Soviet sympathies
was highly welcome. This convergence of interests and, probably
also of personalities, tends to lend weight to Maoist charges that
P'eng and Khrushchev had a close relationship and were up to some-
thing, although exactly what has never been made clear. Here, for
example, is one formulation of this charge:

> Khrushchev highly relished what P'eng Teh-huai did and
> did his best to support P'eng in staging a counterrevo-
> lutionary coup. On July 14, 1959, P'eng produced an
> anti-Party revisionist program at Lushan. Immediately
> before this, on July 8, Khrushchev delivered a speech
> in Poznan of Poland launching an open attack against
> our people's communes. During the Lushan meeting,
> Soviet revisionist diplomatic personnel many times tried
> to get news about the conference. At a reception on
> Army Day on August 1, the Acting Chief Adviser of the
> Soviet revisionists greatly praised P'eng Teh-huai.
> Afterward, Khrushchev again publicly described P'eng
> Teh-huai as being "correct and brave" and as his "best
> friend." They thus supported and cooperated with each
> other . . . [41]

Whatever the nature and precise purpose of this "cooperation,"
there is no doubt that it critically compromised P'eng's position, and
evidently became one of the key factors in his downfall. Despite the
fact that P'eng was no less patriotic and nationalistic than his colleagues, or perhaps because of it, he apparently failed to appreciate
the degree to which he became vulnerable as a result of his contacts
with the Soviets. Looking at these contacts from the standpoint of
his responsibility for China's defense, P'eng also apparently failed to
appreciate the sensitivity of the Chinese leadership on this issue, and

the tactical skill of Mao and his other opponents in exploiting it against him.

This sensitivity probably accounts, to a large extent, for the vehemence of Mao's reaction, and the severity of the Party's censure of P'eng. For such a reaction hardly seems to have been warranted by P'eng's critique alone. Despite their harshness, P'eng's "Letter of Opinion" and other known remarks at Lushan, given the practice of inner-Party democracy, scarcely lead to the conclusion that P'eng headed a "right opportunist anti-Party clique," and that his activities were "fraught with danger for the future of the Party and the People's Liberation Army."[42]

If, however, P'eng's attack was coordinated in any way with the Soviets, then it acquired a totally different coloration and assumed implications which went far beyond the framework of an economic critique. In this case, P'eng's move meant that, for whatever reason, he had conspired with the detested Soviet leader at a time when the Soviets were pressing the Chinese to accept what Mao and many other Chinese leaders regarded as an inferior and humiliating position in their relationship. Thus, at a time when Mao was moving toward an assertion of China's independence from the Kremlin, P'eng appeared to be moving in the opposite direction. If P'eng looked upon himself as the guardian of China's strategic interests, Mao looked upon him as an accomplice of Khrushchev in the Soviet effort to meddle in the internal affairs of the Chinese leadership. This is precisely how Mao depicted P'eng's activities when he justified P'eng's ouster to the Military Affairs Committee shortly after the Lushan Plenum:

> We can never betray the fatherland and work hand-in-
> glove with a foreign country. You comrades have met
> to criticize and repudiate this thing because all of you
> belong to the Communist Party and are Marxists. The
> sabotage of one group by another can never be tolerated.
> We forbid Party members of China to undermine the
> Party organization of another country . . . At the
> same time, we are also not permitted to sow discord
> behind the back of the Central Committee according
> to the bidding of a foreign country.[43]

Such charges clearly struck a responsive cord among the nationalistic Chinese leaders. Consequently, they rallied behind Mao against P'eng even though many of them clearly agreed with the substance of P'eng's economic criticisms. [44] Once P'eng's connection with the Soviets had been established, his dismissal and denunciation became imperative not only as an intra-Party disciplinary measure, but, more importantly perhaps, as a signal to the Kremlin that the Chinese leadership remained united in its determination to persist in the course set by Mao.

Thus, if the above attempt to reconstruct P'eng's motives and calculations has any validity, the conclusion is that P'eng grossly misread the mood of his colleagues. By trying to draw together two antagonistic constituencies, he drove away the more important one--his colleagues. As a result, P'eng and his associates ended up isolated.

Contributing to this isolation were P'eng's political tactics. Although it is far from clear what P'eng was up to, it appears that he had lined up backstage support for his views in order to confront Mao with the backing of a group behind him. [45] P'eng had, in short, formed a faction. This, however, broke the rules of the political game as conducted, at least until the Cultural Revolution, at the highest rungs of the Chinese leadership hierarchy. Voicing opposing viewpoints was an acceptable form of dissent; covertly organizing support for such viewpoints was not. [46] Although the style of P'eng's actions was, of course, much less serious than their substance, it also apparently figured in his dismissal. As Liu Shao-ch'i reportedly said in January 1962, when the P'eng Teh-huai Affair again came up for discussion in Party leadership circles:

> Verdicts can be reversed on those who hold similar viewpoints to P'eng Teh-huai's but who have no illicit relations with foreign countries . . . these comrades are different from P'eng Teh-huai in that . . . they had not organized an anti-Party clique or wanted to usurp the Party. [47]

If P'eng had been able to mobilize support for his position among members of the Central Committee outside his small group of associates, this support was doubtless dissipated by Mao's reaction to his attack. For Mao elevated P'eng's assault on the policies of the Great Leap Forward to the level of a direct challenge to his personal leadership. And on this level, the Chairman was invulnerable.

This reaction, it may be assumed, was triggered by two sets of factors, one personal, the other political. On the personal level, there is no doubt that Mao was deeply stung by P'eng's attack. Nowhere was this more apparent than in his response, made on July 23, to P'eng's critique. Highly personal in tone, this response consisted of a rambling, emotional, and partially incoherent talk in which Mao defended the Great Leap Forward, berated his critics, and warned dramatically that should the army refuse to back him, he would retreat to the countryside and organize a new peasant army.[48] The reason for such an intense reaction is not hard to see. To Mao, the Great Leap Forward was postrevolutionary China's finest hour, an hour which glowed with the promise that Chinese society could be bent to Mao's utopian vision. In the attempt to translate this promise into reality Mao felt, as he told his colleagues, a profound sense of personal involvement and responsibility.[49] And it was this attempt that P'eng, echoing the scorn which emanated from the Kremlin, attacked. Mao could not have demanded less than his dismissal and denunciation.

P'eng's dismissal was doubtless deemed essential by Mao on other grounds as well. First, as has been observed, P'eng and his supporters remained the final stumbling block to the adoption of Maoist strategic and military policies; his dismissal would not only remove the chief spokesman of the professional officers, but would also serve as a warning to these officers. Second, in his broad-ranging opposition to the Maoist concept of "politics in command," P'eng seemed to appear not only as the spokesman for the professional military, but as the archetype of the professionally-oriented leaders whose whole approach to national affairs conflicted basically with the principles which underlay the Great Leap Forward. P'eng, in short, had cast doubt on the Maoist vision of society, a vision which was inseparable from Mao's personal leadership.

Whatever the precise combination of motives that led Mao to link P'eng's policy critique with his personal leadership, it was obviously successful in swaying Party leaders who, in Mao's words, were "wavering . . . at so critical a juncture."[50] For by elevating the confrontation to this level, Mao invoked his unique charismatic appeal and his personal standing in the Party. In effect, Mao presented his colleagues with a package deal: they had to endorse his policies and his leadership, or they had to reject both. This second alternative was unacceptable to the Party leaders.

Consequently, the Lushan Plenum reaffirmed the Party's support for Mao, and condemned P'eng and his associates. In a Resolution adopted on August 16, 1959, by the Eighth Plenum, P'eng and his group were charged with carrying on anti-Party activities in "purposive, prepared, planned, and organized" fashion. "For all his outward pretensions of support for the general line and for Comrade Mao Tse-tung," the Resolution said, P'eng, in fact, opposed "the high-speed development of the national economy" as well as "putting politics in command." Despite this, the Central Committee decided that "the Party should continue to adopt an attitude of great sincerity and warmth towards P'eng Teh-huai and help him recognize and rectify his mistakes."[51]

The inclusion of this last passage in the Central Committee's Resolution suggests two things. First, that the Central Committee was not entirely at ease with its denunciation of P'eng's economic critique. This unease is understandable since many leaders obviously shared P'eng's views, and since the same Plenum which condemned P'eng also had to admit that the economic targets and claims of the Great Leap had been grossly exaggerated. The second conclusion that emerges from the Central Committee's attitude toward P'eng is that his contacts with the Soviets, whatever their purpose and nature, were not regarded as high treason, but as a mistake in judgement on P'eng's part. For had P'eng been guilty of "betrayal" in the usual sense of this term, his fate would have certainly been different. As it was, although P'eng and his associates were removed from their posts, P'eng was not deprived of his freedom and, in fact, was even able to engage in political activities.

Thus ended the drama at Lushan. But the disintegration of the consensus that had marked leadership relations until the Great Leap Forward had just begun. If this attempt to reconstruct the P'eng Teh-huai Affair at the Eighth Plenum has any merit, then it follows that the unity which resulted in the denunciation of P'eng rested not on a policy consensus among China's leaders with respect to the issues of national development raised by P'eng, but on more immediate and compelling considerations: P'eng's relations with the Soviets, and Mao's personal leadership and prestige. These considerations served to submerge divisions within the leadership which derived from the shortcomings of the Great Leap Forward. Following the conclusion of the P'eng Teh-huai Affair, these divisions, no longer held in check by the considerations which were operative at Lushan, came to the fore and began to erode the unity of the Leadership. The erosion of this unity is the story of the first half of the 1960s.

The Period of Retreat

Immediately following the Lushan Plenum, the Party launched a virulent campaign against "rightist opportunists," which, without referring to P'eng and his accomplices by name, refuted the views that P'eng had expressed. This refutation was accompanied by a ringing reaffirmation of the correctness of the Maoist policies which lay behind the Great Leap Forward.[52] The campaign against the "rightists" seemed to have claimed very few victims at the top levels of leadership, but at the lower levels a considerable number of officials were apparently removed.[53]

Not only did the Party reaffirm Mao's policies, but it went to unusual lengths to heap adulation on the Chairman's personal leadership, and to glorify him as "the most outstanding contemporary revolutionary statesman and theoretician of Marxism-Leninism."[54] Since events were soon to show that many of Mao's top colleagues were by this time anything but firm believers in Mao's wisdom, it may be assumed that they praised Mao for reasons other than the stated one of faith in the Chairman. And, in fact, they had good reasons for rallying behind Mao and presenting a solid united front. For one thing, P'eng's attack at Lushan made it necessary to bolster Mao's position and to restore confidence in his judgement, a need that was underscored by the approaching economic crisis. For another, in elevating Mao and his ideology to new heights, the Chinese ruling group undoubtedly had one eye on the Kremlin, for at this time the Chinese were heading toward a major escalation in their dispute with the Soviets: they would soon shift from a criticism of Soviet policies to a criticism of Soviet leadership of the bloc, a shift which, by implication, would establish Mao's claim to this leadership.

Beneath this public display of unity, however, there were undercurrents of tension. One indication of this was revealed by the publication in September 1960 of the Fourth Volume of Mao's Selected Works. Ostensibly meant to be a high point in the campaign to propagate Mao's thought, the publication of this volume also had an inner meaning relevant to leadership relations. The articles in the volume, although dealing with the civil war (1945-1949), were apparently designed by Mao and his supporters to convey a two-fold message to the top leaders. First, it was intended as a reminder of Mao's singular contribution to the achievement of the victory that had brought the Communists to power. More importantly, it was intended to underscore the fact that in the policy debates which took place within the leadership during the period covered by the Fourth Volume, Mao, who took a long-range view, had been proven right by events, whereas leaders who held opposing views had been proven wrong.[55] If this was indeed the message which Mao and his supporters wanted to convey, there can be little doubt that it was prompted by doubts about his approach, doubts which had been raised and repressed at Lushan, but which evidently deepened as the situation deteriorated.

And it deteriorated dramatically. By the autumn of 1960, it was clear that China was in the throes of a severe economic crisis. This crisis inflicted suffering such as the Chinese people had not known under the Communist regime. Agricultural production plummeted and food was in short supply throughout the country. Malnutrition became widespread and famine, unheard of since 1949, hit a number of areas. Basic commodities were extremely difficult, and in some places impossible, to obtain. Industry plunged into a recession, many plants ground to a halt, and a large part of the labor force was thrown out of work.[56] In short, the Great Leap Forward brought disaster. And this disaster was exacerbated by natural calamities as well as by the abrupt withdrawal of all Soviet aid, as a result of the sharpening of the Sino-Soviet conflict.

Less spectacular in its outward manifestations, but no less severe in its implications was the crisis of confidence in the regime, which was engendered in large part by the economic hardships. For these hardships painfully demonstrated to the Chinese people that their leaders, far from infallible, were capable of making monumental and costly blunders. Until the Great Leap Forward the regime had accumulated a vast fund of confidence as a result of its successes during the first decade of rule, and it drew on this fund when it called upon the people to struggle and to sacrifice. The people, on their part, generally responded willingly, if not enthusiastically, and as the Great Leap convincingly demonstrated, were prepared to make the most strenuous efforts on behalf of the goals set forth by the regime. The collapse of the Great Leap Forward, however, shattered the confidence of the people in the leadership. For instead of a better tomorrow, it brought a bitter today. The result was not only physical hardships, but also a mood of demoralization and distrust. This mood led to a breakdown of discipline such as had not been seen in China since the Communists came to power, as individuals struggled for survival in a climate of cynicism and lost confidence.[57]

Confronted with the most severe crisis they had yet faced as rulers of China, the leaders responded with a radical shift of course. This shift got underway piecemeal while the Great Leap was still in progress, but was sharply accelerated in 1960 and was officially sanctioned as the new national policy by the Ninth Plenum of the Central Committee in January 1961. The new slogan put forth by the Plenum, "readjustment, consolidation, filling out, and raising standards," reflected a sober assessment of the situation, and was a far cry from the euphoric catch-phrases of the Great Leap Forward, such as "going all-out to achieve greater, faster, better, and more economical results." But the main difference between the two periods lay not so much in the regime's pronouncements as in its policies.

The policies put into effect after 1960 in effect jettisoned the utopian programs of the Great Leap Forward. These policies encompassed every sphere of Chinese life, but were most pronounced in the economic field. In the agricultural sector, the communes were decentralized, material rewards were reinstituted, private plots were returned to the peasants, and rural free markets were reopened. In industry, quality rather than quantity was reemphasized, the authority of managers in relation to political cadres was reaffirmed, rational planning and coordination were restored, and material incentives were stressed again. Throughout society political pressures and demands were reduced.[58]

. The hallmark of these policies was that they were governed primarily by pragmatic and materialistic considerations rather than by political and ideological criteria. In essence, any measure that contributed to pulling China out of the crisis was acceptable, even if it diverged in vital respects from Maoist principles. "Any cat that can catch mice is a good cat," Teng Hsiao-p'ing is supposed to have said, "be it white or black."[59] This summed up the new approach in a nutshell. Viewed in terms of the visions and techniques of the Great Leap, there can be little doubt that this approach was tantamount to a great retreat. Arching over all the concrete manifestations of this retreat was the dominant fact that it was squarely opposed to the fundamental elements of Mao's thought, as embodied in the Great Leap Forward, and as enunciated with increasing intensity by the Maoists after the Tenth Plenum of September 1962. From the perspective of Mao's growing rift with the Party, it is pertinent to single out three interrelated elements of Mao's thought and their implications. [60]

First, there is Mao's basic belief that "class contradictions" continue to exist in a socialist society even after the socialization of its economic infrastructure. The source of these contradictions is ideological, because the socialist transformation of the economy does not automatically lead to the eradication of bourgeois ideology. The continued existence of this ideology tends to produce political and social forces which threaten to erode the gains of the revolution. In order to protect itself, socialist society has to wage a relentless "class struggle" against capitalist ideology and the socio-political forces to which this ideology gives rise. This "struggle" is inseparably tied to the concept of "uninterrupted revolution," for in Mao's view only by pushing the revolutionary effort forward continously can the resurgence of opposing forces be stemmed. On the other hand, a prolonged respite will inevitably lead to backsliding.

Second, there is Mao's populist faith in the superiority of the subjective "human element" over objective material elements in determining the outcome of the revolutionary struggle, be it the struggle against opposing political and ideological forces, or the struggle against nature. In order to tap the potential inherent in the "human element" the masses must participate in the political process, and must be given wide scope for spontaneous self-expression. Society, therefore, has to be organized in a manner which will facilitate such participation. It must resist trends, such as bureaucratization, specialization, and social stratification, which foster elitism and stifle mass action and initiative.

Third, there is Mao's abiding conviction that the energy and enthusiasm of the masses have to be aroused and channeled to the attainment of collective goals through the inculcation of the individual with the proper values. Put simply, these values can be identified as struggle, sacrifice, selflessness, and a spartan life style-- all in the broader interest of the collective as embodied and expressed by the Chairman and by the qualified interpreters of his thought. Once these values are internalized by the individual, they will not only create the motivation necessary for developing China by relying primarily on the "human element"; they will also ensure that this development will not result in the dilution of revolutionary goals. In the final analysis, therefore, the future of the Chinese revolution is contingent upon the transformation of the individual. Concretely this means that the cultivation of the Maoist values through continuous political indoctrination must be given the highest priority among the goals of the regime.

Since these elements of Mao's thought had been put into practice in the Great Leap Forward, it is pertinent to ask to what extent the failure of the Great Leap affected Mao's belief in them. The answer, as best as can be determined, is that it had very little affect. For Mao simply did not view the Great Leap Forward as a failure--certainly not in the same manner that many of his colleagues did. True, he admitted that mistakes were made. But he viewed these essentially as mistakes in implementation, to be attributed to lower-level cadres, rather than mistakes in policy, which stemmed from basic principles, and for which he took the primary responsibility. Replying to P'eng Teh-huai at Lushan, Mao said:

> The "Communist wind" was principally whipped up by cadres at the hsien and commune level, especially some commune cadres who fleeced the production brigades and teams. This was bad and was not welcomed by the masses . . . The chief reason was that the cadres did not know which was ill-gotten wealth. They were unable to draw a clear line of demarcation, and had not studied political economy. They did not understand what was the law of value, exchange of equal value, or distribution according to work. They were made to see the light in a few months' time.[61]

In his speech to the Tenth Plenum of the Central Committee in September 1962, Mao again ascribed the excesses of the Great Leap Forward to faulty execution of policy:

> In 1959 and 1960, some wrong moves were made principally because the majority of people had no experience in the assessment of problems. The chief trouble was the high rate of requisitioning, and although actually there was not so much grain, it was arbitrarily alleged that there was. Things were blindly directed both in agriculture and industry. A number of mistakes were also made through taking up work on a large scale.[62]

If Mao remained committed to the principles which lay behind the Great Leap Forward, the policies of retreat must have been distasteful to him. For where Mao stressed "class struggle" and permanent revolution, these policies favored retrenchment, stabilization, and gradualism. Where Mao stressed mass mobilization and participation, they bred bureaucratism and elitism. Where Mao stressed utopian social values, they fostered individualism and materialsm. From Mao's viewpoint, in short, the policies of retreat represented a dire threat to the future of the Chinese revolution--"his" revolution.[63] As the Maoists described these policies in the highly charged language of the Cultural Revolution:

> If things had developed according to . . . [the] counter-
> revolutionary revisionist line, drastic class differentiation
> would have occured in the countryside; new bourgeois
> elements would have appeared in great numbers in the
> cities; the masses of workers and poor lower-middle
> peasants would have had a second dose of suffering and
> sunk back into the miserable life of slaves and beasts of
> burden; our country's socialist economic base would
> have been utterly destroyed; a complete change would
> have taken place in the nature of the proletarian state
> power and history would have been turned back on to
> the old road leading to a semicolonial, semifeudal
> society.[64]

Despite the fact that the Maoists regarded the policies of retreat as destructive of the revolution, Mao tolerated these policies for more than two years. Does this mean then that Mao had been shunted aside by his colleagues and deprived of real power? Although the evidence is meager and somewhat ambiguous, on balance this does not seem to have been the case, if "deprived of real power" is taken to mean that the policies of 1960-1962 were carried out despite Mao's opposition to these policies. There is no doubt, to be sure, that Mao's personal authority and prestige at the highest levels of the Party were eroded by the collapse of the Great Leap Forward, an erosion which, as will be seen, was most dramatically reflected in the esoteric attacks leveled at Mao and his policies by intellectuals who had close links with some of the top Party leaders. There are, moreover, indications that in the aftermath of the Great Leap Mao retreated from a close involvement in the day-to-day affairs of the Party.[65] Although it is not clear to what extent this retreat resulted from his own desire or from the design of his colleagues, it is con-

ceivable that had Mao tried to impose policies which ran counter to
the views of Party leaders who controlled the organizational levers
of power in the Party, he would have been blocked at the level of
implementation by these leaders. This, of course, is what happened
increasingly after the Tenth Plenum in September 1962.

Before Mao could be blocked on the level of policy implementation, however, he had to initiate policies which conflicted with the
views of other Party leaders. And this, as far as can be ascer-
tained on the basis of the available evidence, Mao did not do until
the Tenth Plenum. It is not likely, moreover, that Mao was pre-
vented by his colleagues from initiating such policies, for throughout
the years preceding the Cultural Revolution he proved himself able
to intervene in the policy-making process at critical junctures, and
to have the Party adopt decisions in line with his demands. What
this suggests is that until the Tenth Plenum Mao approved these
policies and made no apparent attempt to change them. The main
reason for this, it may be assumed, was that Mao, always a realist
in the face of adversity, was well aware that a major policy shift
was required in order to overcome the post-Great Leap crisis. In
retrospect, however, it is clear that Mao was prepared to accept
the retreat only as a limited and tactical measure. What he was not
prepared to accept was the extent to which the policies put into effect
by key Party leaders departed from his revolutionary blueprint, and
their attempt to pursue these policies on a permanent basis. These
differences between Mao and other leaders, however, did not begin
to surface until 1962. Up to that time Mao does not appear to have
challenged the policies of retreat or tried to reverse them. In fact,
even during the Cultural Revolution the Maoists attributed the measures taken during this period to the Chairman himself:

> From 1960 to 1962, due to natural calamities and the
> sabotage of the Soviet revisionists, China encountered
> temporary economic difficulties. Our great leader
> Chairman Mao adopted a series of effective measures
> to lead the whole Party and the people of the whole
> country to fight against natural calamities and the
> class enemies. [66]

It appears, therefore, that the surface unity achieved at the
Lushan Plenum was maintained at the top level of leadership during
the period of retreat, held together by the imperatives of the crisis
and a basic accord on the policies needed to overcome it. But beneath the surface, the tensions that had burst forth during the P'eng

Teh-huai Affair continued to build up during this period, eroding the cohesion of the leadership.

Specific signs of these tensions are not easily detectable in the Party literature of this period. Although hints are not lacking, [67] they are too vague and veiled to cast much light on the true state of leadership relations. The reason for this probably lies in the policy consensus which prevailed among the central leaders after the collapse of the Great Leap Forward. As long as Mao did not upset this consensus by pressing for major changes, the policy disagreements which would increasingly divide the leadership following the Tenth Plenum did not as yet solidify sufficiently to polarize the ruling group. But in retrospect it is clear that the loss of confidence in Mao and his policies, from which these disagreements would spring, was already widespread at the top level of the ruling heirarchy.

It is symptomatic of the opaqueness enveloping interpersonal relations among the top leaders after the Great Leap that the most concrete clues to this shaken confidence were contained not in the major Party publications, but in the relatively obscure writings of several members of Peking's intellectual community. Employing time-honored techniques of historical allusions and esoteric language, the hidden meaning of which could be understood only in select circles, these intellectuals bitterly blasted Mao's policies, and even went so far as to level scathing and scornful criticism at the Chairman himself. Since these intellectuals did not operate in a political vacuum, there can be little doubt that their writings had significant implications for the power relations between Mao and his colleagues.

Perhaps the most famous attack on Mao produced during this period, though far from the most extreme, was the play The Dismissal of Hai Jui, which was published in January 1961 by Wu Han, a leading intellectual and deputy-major of Peking. Set in the Ming dynasty, the play told the story of a conscientious official, Hai Jui, who, moved by the suffering inflicted on the peasants by the confiscation of their land by corrupt officials, criticized the Emperor for tolerating these abuses and implored him to return their land. For his bold and forthright action, Hai Jui was dismissed from office. With the advantage of hindsight, it is not hard to see the symbolism of the play: if P'eng Teh-huai is substituted for Hai Jui and Mao for the Emperor, the play can be interpreted as an attack on Mao's high-handed and unjust treatment of P'eng, whose misdeed was his expression of concern for the plight of the peasantry. [68]

If the symbolism of Wu Han's play is obvious, his motives for writing it are not. During the campaign against him at the start of the Cultural Revolution, the Maoists attributed far-reaching and sinister political implications to the play. As one charge said of the play:

> It directed its spearhead precisely against the Lushan meeting and against the Central Committee of the Party headed by Comrade Mao Tse-tung, with a view to reversing the decisions of that meeting. The clamorous message of the drama was that the dismissal of the "upright official Hai Jui" in other words of the Right opportunists, was "unfair" and that the Right opportunists should come back to administer "court affairs," that is, to carry out their revisionist program. It was then the urgent desire of the author to support a Right opportunist comeback and resumption of office so as to bring about the restoration of capitalism.[69]

Whether or not Wu Han's play was, in fact, part of a behind-the-scenes effort to "reverse the verdict" on P'eng Teh-huai is not clear. But even if this was not the case, it is clear that the play was loaded with political dynamite. For, at the very least, it constituted a caustic criticism of Mao's leadership on a highly sensitive issue, and there is no doubt that Mao viewed the play precisely in this fashion. As he reportedly said: "The crux of 'Hai Jui Dismissed From Office' is the question of dismissal from office. Emperor Chia Ching dismissed Hai Jui from office. In 1959 we dismissed P'eng Teh-huai from office. And P'eng Teh-huai is 'Hai Jui' too."[70] That Mao did not forgive or forget was, of course, borne out by the fact that it was the resistance of key Party leaders to the purge of Wu Han in the autumn of 1965 that set off the Cultural Revolution.

If Wu Han's writings were volatile politically, they were a "gentle breeze" when compared with the writings of Teng T'o, a secretary of the Peking Party Committee and the official in charge of cultural life in the capital. In some 150 columns which he authored and coauthored in three Peking papers over a period of almost two years, Teng carried out what the Maoists claimed was "an all-out and venomous attack on our great Party, using ancient things to satirize the present, reviling one thing while pointing to another, and making insinuations and oblique thrusts."[71] In retrospect it is clear that this charge was more than justified. For in satirical language that was saturated with scorn,

Teng T'o did indeed denounce Maoist internal and external policies. The Great Leap Forward, Teng said, was nothing more than "boasting and bragging," "completely substituting illusion for reality," "running one's head against the brick wall of reality," and "indulging in fantasy."[72] As for Mao's foreign policies, Teng dismissed Mao's concept that "the East Wind prevails over the West Wind" as a "cliche" and "great empty talk," and, for good measure, advocated reconciliation with the Soviet Union.[73]

More stunning than the assaults on Mao's policies, were the vicious but veiled attacks on Mao himself. Under the guise of telling historical tales, Teng T'o blasted the Maoist concepts underlying the Great Leap Forward and blamed Mao himself for the blunders of the Great Leap. In one column, for example, he criticized Mao's reliance on mass mobilization and implied that the Chairman did not understand the "objective laws" of development:

> As far back as the period of the Spring and Autumn
> Annals and the Warring States and thereabout, there
> were many great statesmen who understood the impor-
> tance of treasuring labor power . . . Through the
> experience of their rule, they discovered the "limits"
> on the "expenditure" of the people's labor power; in
> fact, they discovered certain objective laws governing
> the increase and decrease of labor power . . . If a
> man of the 7th century B.C. understood this truth, we
> who live in the sixties of the twentieth century should
> naturally understand it even better.[74]

In other, much more devastating columns, Teng intimated that Mao was "impractical," "immodest," "rejected good advice," suffered from amnesia, and generally was not in complete control of his senses.[75] Teng's pointed advice to Mao was to "take a complete rest and say nothing and do nothing."[76]

These few examples do not begin to suggest the range and rage of the esoteric criticism directed at Mao and his policies by Teng T'o, Wu Han, and others during this period. But they seem sufficient to raise several central questions: What accounted for the ability of the intellectuals to pursue such activities? What were the implications of these activities for the personal and power relations among the top leaders? Why did Mao and his supporters tolerate the criticisms? Given our scanty knowledge of what really went on in the inner coun-

cils of the Chinese leadership during this period, any attempt to
answer these questions must be speculative and inferential.

As a point of departure, it seems reasonable to reject the notion that the boldness of the intellectuals who produced such blasphemy
can be explained in the context of the freer intellectual and academic
climate which prevailed during the period of retreat. For although
the reins of intellectual control were indeed loosened considerably
during these years, it is inconceivable that any writer in China would
be so naive as to suppose that the parameters of permissiveness ex-
tended to such attacks on Mao's policies, let alone on Mao himself.
This is especially true of writers like Teng T'o who, far from being
an ivory-tower academic (if, indeed, any academic in China could be
characterized in this fashion), was a hardheaded political realist,
finely attuned to the political winds of the day.

Nor is it likely that the writers dared to mount their attacks on
Mao because these attacks were couched in extremely esoteric forms
and they therefore could assume that their real intentions would be
understood only by a small group of like-minded intellectuals, while
the men in power would be unaware of what they were up to. It need
hardly be emphasized that the use of esoteric language as a medium
for political messages is characteristic both of Chinese tradition and
Communist practice, and the men in power are highly sensitive to
such language. While it is true that the attacks on Mao appeared in
fairly obscure publications and, hence, were known to relatively few
people, there can be little doubt that these people included members
of China's ruling elite. In sum, the answer to the activities of China's defiant intellectuals must be sought neither in their naiveté, nor
in the ignorance of the political leaders.

Part of the answer may lie in the assumption that the attacks
of the intellectuals stemmed simply from a gut reaction to the shock
generated by the post-Great Leap crisis, a shock which moved them
to vent their fury at Mao without much thought for the consequences.
Such a reaction, moreover, may have been buttressed by their mis-
judgement (as it turned out later) of the extent to which Mao's authority
had been undermined by the failure of the Great Leap. However, given
the political sensitivity of these writers, and given their lack of an independent power base, which made them completely vulnerable, the
above explanations could hardly have been more than minor contributing
factors to their activities. The main reason, therefore, must be sought
in the realm of power politics, and it could have only been this: the

Chinese writers dared to attack Mao, and were able to publish their attacks over a prolonged period, because they knew that the sentiments which they expressed in their Aesopian tales were shared by some key Party figures who, at the very least, countenanced their activities, and on whom they thought they could rely for protection.

One such figure was P'eng Chen. Holding an impressive array of powerful posts--Mayor of Peking and First Secretary of its Party Committee, Member of the Politburo, and Secretary of the Party Central Committee--P'eng was undoubtedly one of the most influential men in the Chinese power hierarchy.[77] It was in his key bailiwick, which the Maoists later labelled, with good reason, his "independent kingdom," that most of the attacks on Mao appeared, and it is inconceivable that P'eng was not aware of these publications. It is inconceivable, moreover, that these writings could have been published without at least P'eng's tacit approval. And such approval, it may be safely assumed, was given by P'eng because he shared the deep disillusionment of his writer-officials with the policies of the Great Leap Forward.[78]

This assumption is strongly substantiated by P'eng's alleged activities following the collapse of the Great Leap. According to Red Guard sources, in May 1961 P'eng Chen initiated a series of investigations by members of the Peking Municipal Committee into all aspects of the Party's activities during the Great Leap Forward. The purpose of these investigations, the Red Guards charged, was to highlight the "shortcomings" and "mistakes" of the Central Committee in order "to impose all of them on the person of Chairman Mao."[79] Whatever the real intent of these investigations, their results, as expected, amounted to a devastating criticism of the Great Leap.[80]

In November 1961 P'eng Chen allegedly decided that a more systematic inquiry into the operations of the Party during the previous few years was in order. Summoning one of his subordinates, P'eng Chen reportedly told him:

There were quite a number of problems in work in the past few years. The chief reason was that some undertakings had been started on a large scale without conducting experiments, and this was in contravention of the objective law. Now difficulties are encountered. Although natural calamities are also a cause, yet hotheadedness and inability to cling steadfastly to policy are also an important cause . . . The Peitaiho Con-

ference talked about setting up a framework first for
the people's commune. I don't know what exactly
happened, but every place rose with a roar . . .
Some documents were issued with the comment of an
individual, and it could not be guaranteed that they
were free of problems. You better organize some
people to look through the documents of the Central
Committee to see what problems they have. See what
those hotheaded people have done . . . We must gain
experience and learn lessons from them . . . Find
some sober-minded people who are well acquainted
with facts and are capable of detecting problems.
Teng T'o is responsible for guiding this undertaking. [81]

This instruction sparked the so-called "Grandview House Incident." In the middle of November a group consisting of more than
a dozen members of P'eng's Administration gathered at "Grandview
House" in the Western Suburb Park of Peking, "bringing with them
all documents issued by the Central Committee to the <u>hsien</u> level and
above in 1958 through 1961." The mission of the group was described
to it by Teng T'o:

Many shortcomings, mistakes and problems have emerged
in work these few years. What are the reasons? Natural
calamities are not the most important reason. The fundamental problem was detachment from the masses and sub-
jectivism. In short, the objective law has been contravened
and mistakes in line have been made . . . From where did
the tendency to exaggerate things spring up? This must
be found from among the documents of the Central Committee. We must be bold enough to locate and raise problems from the documents of the Central Committee. All
of you may discuss things in this connection. [82]

This the members of the group apparently proceeded to do with
a vengeance. Their findings bore a close resemblance to P'eng Teh-
huai's Lushan critique. In fact, their accusers said they they "totally
rejected the great significance of the 'Lushan Conference' and its opposition to P'eng Teh-huai's Right opportunist line, and attempted to
reverse the correct decision passed on the Right opportunist." Whether or not this charge is true, the conclusions reached by the "Grandview House" group, as reported by the Red Guards, amounted to a
far-reaching attack on the policies of the Great Leap. Here is a

sampling of the group's comments:

> They talked nonsense, saying: "Chairman Mao thought
> it was easy to accomplish the leap forward in agricul-
> ture and industry, and he was too eager for success."
> They said: "Haste makes waste." What was more
> malicious was that they said that "the Chairman is
> arrogant" and "advanced in years." . . . they said:
> "Why did temporary difficulties appear? An important
> reason was that the Central Committee was feverish and
> the targets were high, and they regarded things as easy
> to accomplish. This was brought about by the opposition
> to Right deviation" . . . They said that the three red
> banners "have violated the law of economic development
> and greatly undermined production" . . . They said there
> was contradiction in greater, faster, better and more eco-
> nomical results, since "greater and faster results cannot
> be better and and more economic ones" . . . They
> smeared self-reliance as "closing the country to trade"
> . . . They talked nonsense, saying that "refining iron
> and steel on a large scale was the view of the leader-
> ship, but not the view of the masses." . . . They
> cried: "The people's commune has been set up pre-
> maturely. There are neither experimental spots nor
> rules and regulations. "[83]

Conclusions such as these were incorporated into a lengthy
report that was submitted to P'eng Chen. What exactly, if anything,
P'eng had intended to do with this report is not clear. According to
Red Guard charges, P'eng had been part of an anti-Mao conspiracy,
but backed out when things began to go sour:

> Counterrevolutionary revisionist P'eng Chen and his sworn
> confederates originally planned to make a surprise attack
> in coordination with Liu Shao-ch'i and Teng Hsiao-p'ing
> at . . . [the January 1962 7,000 cadre meeting]. They
> planned to fire off a large number of anti-Party bullets
> which they had collected over a number of years so that
> they might attain their ulterior criminal objective of
> usurping power in the Party and government. However,
> seeing that Liu Shao-ch'i and Teng Hsiao-p'ing had lost
> the battle . . . [P'eng] retracted his sinister hand to

avoid completely exposing his own counterrevolutionary
features. [84]

Although this charge appears to be wholly trumped up, [85] one
thing seems clear from the Red Guard accounts: the activities of
P'eng Chen and his subordinates, whatever their real intent, resulted from and reflected a profound disaffection with Maoist policies
and, to some extent, with Mao himself. This disaffection, at the
very least, must have strengthened the determination of leaders such
as P'eng Chen not to permit a return to policies which led to the
"mistakes" that his investigations had spotlighted. And it was this
determination that formed the basis for the opposition of top Party
leaders to Mao, when Mao began to press for a return to more revolutionary policies.

Whereas the alienation of P'eng Chen from Mao and his policies
goes a long way toward explaining the sustained activities of Teng T'o
and the other writers who criticized Mao, it does not explain why Mao
tolerated these activities for such a long period. As far as "investigations" of the type that were carried out by the Peking Municipal
Committee are concerned, it is likely that since such activities were
surreptitious, Mao and his associates were not aware of them until
the Red Guard invasion of secret files during the Cultural Revolution.
It is most unlikely, however, that Mao was unaware of the attacks
launched against him in the Peking press and elsewhere. Even if
the Chairman himself did not scan these publications, it may be assumed that his subordinates, especially those concerned with literary
affairs, such as Yao Wen-yuan and Chang Ch'un-ch'iao, brought the
contents of these publications to his attention. And if they did not,
surely Chiang Ch'ing did, for, according to her own testimony, she
acted as "a sort of roving sentry in the field of culture and education." As she described her duties: "What I have been doing is to
subscribe to some magazines and newspapers, to leaf through them
and to pick out materials which I think noteworthy, including positive
and negative materials. I finally submit them to Chairman Mao for
reference. Generally speaking, my work has been carried out in this
way for many years. "[86] In sum, it is reasonable to conclude that
Mao could not have remained ignorant of what went on in China's
intellectual circles. In fact, Mao alluded to the writings of the
defiant intellectuals in his speech to the Tenth Plenum of the Central
Committee in September 1962, vaguely linking these writings to the
political machinations of his opponents. "Isn't the writing of novels
the fashion of the day now?" Mao said. The use of novels to carry

out anti-Party activities is a great invention. To overthrow a political power, it is always necessary first of all to create public opinion,
to do work in the ideological sphere."[87] That Mao was determined
to "settle accounts" with these intellectuals was, of course, demonstrated by the fact that they became the first victims of the Cultural
Revolution.

The question still remains, however, why Mao, as far as
can be determined, did not try to put a stop to the attacks of the
intellectuals until the Tenth Plenum. Or, in the unlikely event
that he did, why was he unsuccessful? It must be stated at the
outset that of all the unanswered questions surrounding this enig-
matic period, this one remains one of the most vexing. For despite its importance for an assessment of the state of power relationship, the evidence is too meager and too contradictory to
permit any convincing conclusions. The most that can be done,
therefore, is to raise hypotheses for consideration.

One hypothesis is that Mao did not immediately launch a
counterattack against the defiant intellectuals because he was simply
incapable of doing so, having been effectively removed from power
by his colleagues in the aftermath of the Great Leap Forward. This
view, however, seems to be superficial and simplified. For although
Mao's power position was doubtless weakened following the collapse
of the Great Leap, there is also evidence to suggest that Mao had
never lost his capacity for exerting a decisive influence on the policy-
making process.[88] The question then is not whether Mao was "in
power" or "out of power," for he was never completely either "in"
or "out," but rather at what level of the exercise of power was he
effective. And it seems that it was at the level of making his will
felt in some of the burgeoning "independent kingdoms" within the vast
Party organization that his effectiveness had been seriously reduced.
If so, it is possible that Mao was unable, or thought himself unable,
to crack down on the dissident intellectuals without bringing the mat-
ter before the Central Committee and launching a major campaign.
And perhaps from this vantage point the time was not ripe to war-
rant such a campaign.

This leads to a second, and interrelated hypothesis, namely
that Mao did not at the time seek a major confrontation with the intellectuals and their protectors because such a confrontation would
have fostered widespread attention on the criticism directed against

him. This criticism, after all, was extremely opaque and was
known to relatively few people. At the height of the economic
crisis engendered by the failure of the Great Leap, and so soon
after the P'eng Teh-huai Affair, it would hardly have been a prudent move on Mao's part to give nationwide publicity to this issue.
True to his combat strategy of choosing his own time for a battle,
Mao held his hand. Why he held it for so long is a question the
answer to which is inextricably intertwined with the whole flow of
events that led to the Cultural Revolution. At the core of these
events was Mao's effort to reassert control over the increasingly
insular and unresponsive power centers within the Party organization. Although there were a number of factors behind this effort,
the attacks of the intellectuals on Mao and his policies must have
played a significant part in demonstrating to Mao the extent to which
his authority had waned in various Party organizations, and must
have raised suspicions in his mind with respect to the personal fi-
delity and revolutionary commitment of some of his top colleagues.
If so, it may be concluded that the attacks of the intellectuals on
Mao, far from being an isolated phenomenon in the intellectual
sphere, had a political significance which made them an integral
and important link in the chain of developments that culminated in
the Cultural Revolution.

To the Tenth Plenum

Regardless of how the attacks of the intellectuals affected Mao's
relations with his top colleagues, there is no doubt that these relations were strained during the period between January and September
1962. For it was during this period that the nascent differences between Mao and his supporters on the one hand, and Liu Shao-ch'i and
other like-minded leaders on the other hand began to surface and to
be aired in Party circles. As has been noted, these differences,
can be traced back to the early years of the People's Republic, and,
in fact, long before that, but there is no doubt that they became
irreconcilable only after the collapse of the Great Leap Forward.
Deriving from the divergent conclusions which the two men and their
supporters drew from the experience of the Great Leap, these differences, as has been shown, were submerged at the Eighth Plenum by
more compelling political considerations, and during the period of
retreat by a basic policy consensus. This consensus, however,
rested on a shaky foundation, as revealed, for instance, in the polit-

ically-significant attacks of the intellectuals on Mao and his policies. Thus, when the leadership began to reappraise its policies and to make plans for the future, the elements of conflict came to the fore. As a result, the consensus that had prevailed at the apex of the power pyramid during the period of retreat began to break down.

The reappraisal of Party policy apparently began at a major conference in late January 1962, which was attended by no less than some 7,000 cadres from the five levels of Party administration (commune, county, district, province, and center). It was evidently at this conference that Liu Shao-ch'i expressed views which could be construed as contradictory to Mao's approach in some important respects. The debates triggered by the reappraisal apparently continued after the January Conference, culminating in the two-month long Peitaiho and Peking Work Conferences, which preceded the landmark Tenth Plenum of the Central Committee. This Plenum apparently brought the debates within the Party to an end, because Mao succeeded in getting the Party to adopt a resolution which called for the revival of "class struggle," thus terminating the period of retreat, and seemingly resolving the differences between Mao and other leaders. In practice, however, these differences were far from resolved, but rather were again hidden behind a facade of unity. After the Tenth Plenum the policy disagreements at the top levels of the Chinese leadership would develop into an organizational conflict that inexorably propelled the Chinese power structure toward the Cultural Revolution.

Although the materials which became available during the Cultural Revolution, especially from Red Guard sources, seem adequate to substantiate the broad framework of leadership relations outlined above, they are woefully inadequate when it comes to filling this framework with concrete contents. What precisely were the specific issues which separated Mao and other leaders? What was the scope and intensity of the conflict between them at various junctures? What exactly were the stages of development of the conflict? These and similar questions cannot be answered in a satisfactory manner on the basis of the available materials. For one thing, these materials represent the Maoist version of a great political struggle in which Mao was the principal protagonist, and although they contain numerous nuggets of "inside" information, they can hardly be expected to present a true picture of the events. For another, in no case, as far as can be determined, do the Red Guard sources provide complete contemporary texts of speeches or reports by leaders who disagreed with Mao

(with the exception of "confessions" and "self-criticisms" given under
the various forms of pressure during the Cultural Revolution). What
they do provide is a windfall of quotations attributed to many top
leaders who purportedly opposed Mao and his policies. While there
is no doubt that in most cases such quotations were taken out of context in order to build the Maoist case against the opposition by iso-
lating the areas of discord, the record of developments, as well as
other indications, [89] strongly suggest that the remarks attributed to
Mao's opponents in fact reflected the thrust, if not always perhaps
the precise wording, of their opinions. Given the inherent limitations
of the source materials, any attempt to reconstruct the development
of the dispute must inevitably be partly speculative, and must allow
for a margin of error in interpretation. And this margin widens in
direct proportion to the analyst's attempt to descend from a high level of generality and to come to grips with the details and dynamics
of the intraleadership conflict.

The growing gulf between Mao and other leaders was apparently
reflected in their speeches at the January Conference. Although the
gulf was as yet nowhere nearly as wide as later portrayed by the
Maoists, there can be little doubt that some of the views voiced by
Liu Shao-ch'i were significantly at variance with Mao's stand. These
views related to the reasons for the collapse of the Great Leap Forward and to the lessons which the Party should draw from this collapse. Referring to the crisis generated by the Great Leap, Liu
asked: "How did such a difficult situation appear? Why was it that
the production of food, cloth, and consumer goods was not increased
but decreased. What is the reason?" He then went on:

> The reason is twofold: One is natural disasters . . .
> The other was that since 1958 we had shortcomings and
> mistakes in our work. I went to a place in Hunan.
> There the peasants said that 30 percent of the difficulties
> were brought about by natural calamities while 70 percent
> were caused by man-made factors. This you have to
> admit. In a number of areas in the country it may be
> said that the difficulties are chiefly attributed to our
> shortcomings and mistakes, and the achievements made
> are far from primary. [90]

Expounding on these "shortcomings and mistakes," Liu criticized
some of the basic principles and practices of the Great Leap Forward:

mass movements, the notion of unbalanced economic growth, the stress on spontaneity, and the people's communes. Without attempting to go into the question to what extent Mao and Liu differed on these issues before the Great Leap and to what extent Liu supported the launching of the Great Leap, [91] there can be little doubt that to Liu and many other top leaders the collapse of the Great Leap and the consequent crisis was a traumatic and sobering experience, which left them convinced of the futility of Mao's methods for modernizing China. This disillusionment was reflected in Liu Shao-ch'i's remarks at the January Conference. With respect to mass movements Liu had this to say:

> In the past few years, instead of saving on the effort of the masses, we have wasted a lot of their energy. This is a very big mistake. Our comrades are worried that the masses may not arouse themselves with zeal. This is a problem which should be properly studied. The reason is that in the past several years the enthusiasm and effort of the masses have been dampened, and in certain places seriously undermined. [92]

And again:

> We have launched many movements in the past several years. Most of these movements were set in motion abruptly. Some were even without official documents; they were set in motion on hearing some not very accurate news. Such a way of doing things is not good. [93]

At the January Conference, Teng Hsiao-p'ing repeated this theme:

> In the past few years we have carried out many large-scale movements. We have even more or less regarded these large-scale movements as the only form of the mass line. It is not good to have a movement every day. [94]

The heaven-storming approach of the Great Leap, which stressed spontaneity and unbridled initiative at the expense of planning and order also came in for sharp criticism by Liu Shao-ch'i:

> With regard to agricultural production, farming systems are changed at random. Some technical measures which

are impractical and unscientific are adopted indiscriminately. Some water conservancy projects which are not
only useless but harmful are built. With respect to industry, rules and regulations are abolished at will and
some impractical and unscientific technical measures are
adopted indiscriminately, with the result that equipment
has been damaged, the quality of certain products has
declined, the costs have increased, and labor productivity
dropped. [95]

The result of the approach which characterized the Great Leap
Forward was disequilibrium between the various sectors of the economy:

As the planned targets of industrial and agricultural
production are too high and the front of capital construction is too long, there have been serious disproportions
between the various sectors of the national economy,
and between consumption and accumulation . . .

. . . In the process of enforcing the general line, at
certain times we look at things one-sidedly. For instance,
we pay attention only to greater and faster results but
pay little or no attention to better and economical results.
We give attention only to quantity but our attention to
variety and quality is insufficient. [96]

Liu's disdain for a high-speed and unsystematic approach to
development was apparent in his comments on the people's commune:

Now it appears that the people's commune should be
operated. The problem is that we must not set up
too many of them at one stroke and go too fast. We
should first conduct experiments to create models and
then gradually set them up in a well-prepared, method-
ical and orderly manner, by separate stages and groups.
Moreover, we must continue to sum up experiences . . .
Herein lies the principal experience and lesson in the
operations of people's communes. [97]

Although Mao did not attempt to shirk responsibility for the policies of the Great Leap Forward, it seems that Liu Shao-ch'i was
prepared to go substantially further than Mao in having the central

leadership accept the blame for the deleterious effects of those policies. As he said at the January Conference:

> The Center takes the view that it is necessary to point
> out . . . that for all these defects and mistakes in
> work over the past several years the Center must pri-
> marily take the responsibility . . . When I say that
> . . . I naturally also mean the various departments
> of the Center, the State Council and its subordinate
> agencies. [98]

Unlike Mao, moreover, Liu clearly implied that the policies of retreat had cleansed the Party body politic of the disease which had afflicted it during the Great Leap Forward:

> In the last few years not a few shortcomings and mis-
> takes have appeared in our work . . . But these . . .
> are now a thing of the past. It seems as if a person
> who has been taken seriously ill is now fully himself
> again. [99]

If this was Liu's diagnosis of China's condition, his prescription for the future was to continue applying the remedy which had worked. This meant that the Party should persist in its pragmatic approach to development, unencumbered by doctrinal restraints and political considerations. This view was succinctly stated by Liu in a speech delivered in June 1962:

> During the period of transition, all methods conducive
> to the arousing of peasants' production enthusiasm may
> be adopted. It is not necessary to say which method
> is the best or the only workable method. The retreat
> in industry must be sufficient, and so must the retreat
> in agriculture. This implies, among other things, giv-
> ing production quotas to the individual households and
> a return to individual farming. [100]

At the January Conference Liu sounded a similar note:

> From now on we must give more attention to better and
> economical results and achieve a leap forward with re-
> spect to variety and quality. We must increase the
> volume of production but we must not chase after quan-

tity only. Henceforth the volume of production need
not necessarily be increased too substantially, but more
attention must be given to variety and quality and to
ancillary projects so that we may carry out construction
independently, on the basis of self-reliance. [101]

Other Party leaders came to similar conclusions. Although we
have been unable to find any record of their speeches at the January
Conference, remarks made by some of the leaders during the policy
debates of 1962 indicate that they expressed views much like those put
forward by Liu with respect to future policy. For example, Teng
Hsiao-p'ing, in a speech delivered in July, also underscored the need
for a hardheaded and gradualist approach. "Whether in industry or
agriculture," he said, "we must walk step by step . . . We may hear
many opinions, but we must not make decisions hastily. Prudence
brings profits and causes less side effects."[102] Chu Teh was more
blunt: "Individual farming," he said, "will not topple socialism."[103]

In sum, it is clear that by 1962 the lines between Mao and the
leaders of what later became the opposition were drawn. But just
how sharply is a moot point. Since Red Guard sources provide only
out-of-context quotations from speeches made by these leaders, it is
impossible to determine the main thrust of any given speech and to
draw up a balance sheet between the areas of agreement and disagreement. Taken cumulatively, these quotations leave no doubt that by
1962 Liu and other leaders were voicing views which were fundamentally incompatible with the Maoist approach. Nor is there any doubt,
from the perspective of hindsight, that these views were pivotal in
propelling Mao toward an open break with his colleagues. But precisely how this conflict developed in the period that began with the
January Conference and ended with the Tenth Plenum (and, needless
to say, thereafter as well) remains an open question.

In the Maoist version of this period, the question is not open at
all. The January Conference, according to the Maoists, was the scene
of a bitter confrontation between Mao and Liu. "At that time," so it
is alleged, "those tortoises and turtles of the bourgeois headquarters
headed by Liu Shao-ch'i came out in full force to launch a frenzied
attack against the Party and socialism. At the enlarged work conference of the Central Committee held in January 1962, Liu Shao-ch'i
came forward in person and launched a frenzied attack against the
Party Central Committee headed by Chairman Mao." In response,
"our great leader Chairman Mao delivered an important speech at

the enlarged conference of the Central Committee . . . This hit the nail on the head and unmasked the counterrevolutionary revisionist essence of Liu Shao-ch'i and a handful of persons, thus sounding the alarm for the whole Party to guard against capitalist restoration."[104]

Available evidence does not substantiate this extreme version of the events. Whatever may have been the balance in Liu's speeches between agreement and disagreement with Maoist policies, the text of Mao's speech at the January Conference hardly indicates that the Chairman launched a counterattack against Liu. In fact, Mao did not address himself directly to Liu's remarks, but rather limited his speech to a general discussion of a number of topics. At most, Mao's speech can be interpreted as a mild refutation of the pragmatically-oriented approach advocated by Liu and others. In this speech Mao defended the rationale behind the Great Leap Forward and glossed over its shortcomings. He berated Party leaders who, he said, were afraid of the masses, and exhorted these leaders to subject themselves to mass criticism. He warned that among the Party members there were "individualists, bureaucrats, subjectivists, and even some backsliders" who "hang up the Party shingle . . . but represent the bourgeoisie." And he sounded a theme which was to gain increasing prominence and significance in the coming months:

> The reactionary classes which have already been over-
> thrown still plot their restoration. In socialist society,
> there may still arise new bourgeois elements. Classes
> and class struggle exist in the entire socialist stage.
> This class struggle is long-lasting, complex, and
> sometimes even violent.[105]

In conclusion it may be suggested that discord between Mao and Liu emerged into the open in Party circles at the January Conference, but it was still, at least in its outward manifestations, subdued and, as far as can be determined, did not overtly affect interpersonal relations among the top leaders.

In view of the fact that Liu Shao-ch'i, and presumably other leaders as well, obviously criticized the Great Leap Forward in a caustic fashion at the January Conference, it is not clear why Mao's response to these criticisms was so low-keyed. One possible reason is that these criticisms were subsumed within a broader framework of agreement, and Mao chose to ignore the negative and to accentuate the positive.[106] This assumption may be inferred from Mao's state-

ment that "at this meeting we have already made a preliminary
summary of past work experience, mainly the experience of the
later four years. This summary reflects the contents of Liu Shao-
ch'i's report."[107] Since it is inconceivable that Mao would put his
stamp of approval on a report which conflicted fundamentally with
his basic views, it is evident that Liu's report was acceptable to
him. And it was acceptable presumably because Liu, in order to
avoid precisely the kind of confrontation that the Maoists now maintain occured, probably went along with Mao in his overall assessment
of the situation, despite his criticism of the Great Leap. As Mao
himself said:

> Comrade Liu Shao-ch'i said in the newspaper that in
> the last four years, our line was correct, our achieve-
> ments were major ones, and if we made some mistakes
> and suffered some losses in our actual work, we gained
> experience and so were stronger and not weaker.[108]

A second related possibility is that Mao chose to overlook Liu's
criticisms at this time on the assumption that Liu and other leaders
would back his views insofar as future policies were concerned. Such
an assumption may have been strengthened by the general thrust of
Liu's speeches which, as has been observed, was probably acceptable
to Mao. If so, then it appears that at the January Conference a
pattern began to emerge which would increasingly characterize leadership relations thereafter. This pattern would find Mao acting on the
premise that he could sway his colleagues, whatever their dissent,
by pressing his views upon them through his statements and directives.
His colleagues, on the other hand, would stop short of bringing their
differences with Mao to a head by open and full-scale opposition to
his directives, but rather would reinterpret or disregard these directives in the course of implementation. And it was this pattern of
leadership relations that kept the frictions between Mao and his colleagues from exploding into open conflict for a relatively long time.

Whether or not this pattern was already operative at the January
Conference, it seems clear that after the conference Liu and other
leaders displayed a dogged disregard for Mao's views and proceeded
to implement their own policies. These policies, it need hardly be
added, were based on the views which Liu and other leaders had
expressed at the January Conference and elsewhere. Foremost among
these policies was the so-called "san-tzu i-pao" policy in agriculture.
Attributed by the Maoists to Liu Shao-ch'i and other top leaders, this

policy postulated the extension of plots for private use, the extension of free markets, the increase in the number of small enterprises with sole responsibility for their profits and losses, and the fixing of output quotas on the basis of individual households.[109] Under the "san-tzu i-pao" system, there were apparently cases in which collective lands were divided among peasants on a long-term basis, and in the interest of increasing production peasants were permitted to neglect work within the communal framework in order to engage in private farming.[110] Although Mao himself had sanctioned the retreat in the agricultural sector--including the decentralization of communes down to the production team level, the increase in the size of the private plots, and the broadening of the incentive structure--the extension of these measures under the "san-tzu i-pao" system in 1962 obviously went too far for the Maoists. While the Maoist charge that this was an "attempt to break up the people's communes and restore capitalism"[111] may be overdrawn, there can be little doubt that the perpetuation of the "san-tzu i-pao" policy would have led to a drastic dilution of collective agriculture.

Despite this, top Party officials had no hesitations about advocating the policy of "san-tzu i-pao." One such official was Ch'en Yun, who had fallen out of favor during the Great Leap presumably because of his opposition to it, but by 1962 had made a comeback as head of the Party's financial group. Ch'en's appointment to this post was made on the recommendation of Liu Shao-ch'i. As Liu explained this in his "self-criticism" in October 1966: "As at the time I over-trusted Ch'en Yun, I listened to his opinions. We had common ground in ideology. I recommended Ch'en Yun to the Center and Chairman Mao to be head of a fiscal group."[112] In this capacity Ch'en convened the "Hsilou Conference" in February 1962, presumably in order to discuss the Third Five-Year Plan. Here is the Maoist version of that Conference:

> In 1962, he schemed for the Liu-Teng sinister head-
> quarters, and convened the "Hsilou Conference." He
> portrayed the situation since 1958 as a "mass of pitch
> darkness," gave exaggerated figures in the state bud-
> get, and attempted to negate fundamentally the three
> red banners. He cast forth the third five-year plan
> and wanted to use it as the Right opportunist program
> for the period of rehabilitation or period of readjust-
> ment. In the countryside, he vigorously advocated
> "distribution of land and fixing of output quotas based
> on the households" and restoration of capitalism.[113]

Ch'en Yun was not alone among the top leaders who proposed such steps during this period of reappraisal. For example, according to Liu Shao-ch'i, Teng Tzu-hui at several conferences advocated giving production quotas to individual households. And "a central comrade" suggested that land be distributed to the households. These opinions, Liu said, opposed the general line and stemmed from a wrong appraisal of the situation. He then went on: "I personally heard the opinion about distribution of land to the households, and I did not refute it. This was a big mistake."

This was not the only "mistake" Liu made during this period.[114] According to the Maoists:

> Between March and May 1962, Liu Shao-ch'i clamored
> that "we have still not clearly understood the difficulties."
> "The present fiscal and economic difficulties are very
> serious." Industrial and farm production "will continue
> to decline;" "there will be disproportions;" "there is
> monetary devaluation," and "our economy is on the
> brink of collapse." He said further: "If we are un-
> willing to admit the difficulties or admit them partially
> out of fear that full explanation . . . would cause the
> cadres to lose their confidence, if we think that we can
> easily solve problems by evading them, and if we do
> not deal with the difficulties seriously but lightly, then
> clearly we have neither the bearing of a true courageous
> revolutionary nor the attitude of a Marxist-Leninist."
> During the past year and up to now, so far as the Center
> is concerned, there has been insufficient assessment of
> the grave situation." "Have we adequately assessed the
> present situation? If we have not, let's assess it
> again."[115]

By the summer of 1962 Mao obviously decided that these "assess-ments" and the policies which they were producing had gone far enough. According to the Maoists, "for the purpose of hitting back at Liu Shao-ch'i and others, Chairman Mao presided over the Work Conference of the Central Committee convened at Peitaiho in August 1962."[116] In the available texts of Mao's two talks at this Conference he named no names, but according to some sources Mao criticized such top economic officials as Ch'en Yun, Li Fu-chun, Li Hsien-nien, Po I-po, and Teng Tzu-hui.[117] Be that as it may, it seems clear from Mao's strident tone that tensions were high at the Peitaiho Conference. Unlike his speech at the January Conference, which seemed to skirt the criticisms raised by his colleagues, at Peitaiho Mao appeared to be refuting these criticisms head on. "Some comrades," Mao said, "consider the past a shaft of light and the present a shaft of darkness without light. Is it or isn't it a shaft of darkness? Which of the two viewpoints is right?" Mao's answer was optimistic: "Let's go back to the three phrases of the Lushan conference of 1959: 'The accomplishments are great; the problems are not few; the future is bright.'" Mao conceded, however, that some people thought otherwise: "The thought of some men is confused. They have no future and they've lost faith. That's not right."[118]

Mao then raised the issue of growing class differentiations in the countryside:

> In the final analysis, will we take the socialist road or the capitalist road? Will the rural cooperativization go on? Will we have "production contracted by the household" or collectivization? . . . We now have independent landholders. The remnants of the landlords and rich peasants still exist . . . The landlord and rich peasant remnant bourgeoisie vie with the petty bourgeoisie to be independent landholders.

If the proletariat did not take heed of these developments, Mao warned, it would be impossible to consolidate the collective economy and "capitalism may prevail."[119]

In another talk, Mao returned to this theme and again warned of the dangers of "revisionism" in the economy, especially in the agricultural sector. But he reserved his most caustic comments for the Party bureaucracy. A large number of Party members, Mao said, were "petty bourgeoisie"; some had never been "remolded" and "had no spiritual preparation for the socialist revolution." As for the Party apparatus, Mao complained that the various departments which dealt with economic affairs failed to ask for instructions before they acted and failed to report on their actions afterward. They were out of touch with the Central Committee above and the masses below. They had, in effect, become "independent kingdoms." Mao then went on: "We know all about foreign affairs. We know even what Kennedy is going to do, but who knows what the various departments in Peking are going to do? I just do not know the situation in several major economic departments."[120]

That the political temperature was high at Peitaiho is also indicated by some of Liu Shao-ch'i's remarks in his "self-criticism."[121] Although cryptic, they suggest that by the summer of 1962 the lines between Mao and Liu had become sharply drawn. "At the Peitaiho Conference . . ." Liu said, "I was guilty of the Rightist line," intimating that he had argued for policies which ran counter to Mao's views. And he added that "at the Peitaiho Conference class struggle was brought up for discussion," suggesting that up to that time this had not been a crucial issue. Thus, the simmering difference between Mao and Liu, which had begun to come to the fore at the January Conference, crystallized in the subsequent months and came to a head at the Peitaiho Conference. Although the intensity of the dispute at this Conference cannot be determined, it must have seriously strained the interpersonal relations at the pinnacle of the power pyramid. Further contributing to these strains were two issues which touched sensitive nerves in the Party organism: the question of P'eng Teh-huai, which was raised again during this period, and the publication of the revised edition of Liu Shao-ch'i's tract on "Self-Cultivation."

The question of P'eng Teh-huai was apparently raised openly at the January Conference by officials who felt that the time had come to "reverse the verdict" on P'eng. The details surrounding this episode, as almost every episode that occured during this period, are obscure, but on the basis of circumstantial evidence it is possible to speculate on the reasons which led to the effort to rehabilitate P'eng and other officials who were purged during the "anti-Rightist" campaign. Already at the Lushan Plenum, as has been pointed out, many officials apparently agreed with the substance of P'eng's criticisms, and they rallied behind Mao against him due to other considerations. Events after Lushan only underlined the correctness of P'eng's views. Following his dismissal, moreover, P'eng himself had been extremely active, traveling widely and soliciting support for his case.[122] On the other hand, the political and charismatic appeal which Mao had been able to bring to bear in the direct confrontation with P'eng at Lushan had lost much of its force, especially during the hard times of the post-Great Leap Forward crisis.

Despite the apparent existence of widespread sentiment in favor of P'eng Teh-huai, there is no evidence to substantiate the charge put forward by some Maoist publications that at the January Conference Liu Shao-ch'i "flagrantly reversed the verdict on the P'eng Teh-huai Right opportunist anti-Party clique. "[123] What Liu apparently did say at the Conference, and this the Maoist sources in fact conceded, was that P'eng's views had been "in accord with facts in many respects . . . "[124] However, as has already been pointed out, Liu drew a distinct line between P'eng on the one hand and, on the other hand, officials who had shared P'eng's views but had not engaged in activities similar to P'eng's, namely, maintaining "illicit relations" with the Soviet Union or organizing an "anti-Party clique. "[125] With respect to such officials Liu was prepared to be lenient: "If an accused lodges an appeal, and if the leadership and other comrades think this is necessary, the verdict on him can be changed. "[126]

Liu's support for the reconsideration of judgements passed during the anti-Rightist campaign stemmed from his view that during the campaign Party organizations had been given excessive leeway which led to "leftist" deviations. As Liu reportedly said at the January Conference:

> After the Lushan Conference, the anti-Rightist struggle
> was improperly unfolded among the cadres in rural
> area, enterprises, and schools, and even among the
> masses. In many places and departments signs have
> appeared that the anti-Rightist struggle has been aggra-
> vated . . . In recent years some Party organizations
> repeated the mistakes of the struggle that had gone too
> far in the period of the three Leftist lines. [127]

Such excesses were clearly anathema to Liu. For one thing, they ran against the grain of his organizational approach and his basic notion that Party rectification campaigns should be tightly structured and supervised by the leadership. [128] For another, the anti-Rightist campaign probably interfered to some extent with the implementation of the policies of retreat, because many officials most capable of executing these policies were presumably purged, while others were inhibited. Consequently, Liu insisted that all Party organizations guilty of "leftist" mistakes "must promptly rectify them and shall not be allowed to carry out such excessive struggle. They should follow a set of normal standards of inner-Party struggle that have been formed long ago in our Party. "[129] What Liu was saying, in effect, was that the Party should strengthen its organizational discipline, which meant a greater emphasis on "centralism" rather than on "democracy," and should reduce the political tensions which characterized the anti-Rightist

campaign. This approach stood in sharp contrast to Mao's stress
on "extensive democracy" in the Party's organizational life, and to
his calls for the revival of "class struggle."

As a result, Liu's stand on the question of the "reversal of
verdicts" was unacceptable to Mao. Following the January Conference "verdicts" were apparently "reversed" on a large scale; according to one Maoist source, "several thousand Rightists" were
rehabilitated in Anwei province alone. [130] Because of his deep personal involvement in the P'eng Teh-huai Affair, Mao probably viewed
this trend as undermining his authority. The purged officials, moreover, had, after all, opposed his policies to one degree or another,
and Mao probably considered their rehabilitation as endangering the
policies which he espoused. In any event, by the time of the Tenth
Plenum Mao decided to call a halt to this trend. In his speech at
the Plenum Mao insisted on renaming "Right opportunism as revisionism" in China, and then said:

> Recently, there is a tendency to vindicate and rehabil-
> itate people. This is wrong. Only those who have
> been wrongfully charged can be vindicated and rehabil-
> itated, but those who have been correctly dealt with can-
> not be so vindicated. Those who have been wrongfully
> charged must be vindicated in whole or in part as the
> case justifies, but those who have been correctly dealt
> with cannot be vindicated. We cannot vindicate and
> rehabilitate all people. [131]

Liu's desire for increased Party discipline and decreased
stress on "struggle," which partly accounted for his stand on the
issue of rehabilitating "rightists," was also at the core of his now-
infamous revised tract on "Self-Cultivation." Published in a new edition on August 1, 1962, this work did not become a focus of conflict
at the time, but during the Cultural Revolution it became one of the
central planks in the programmatic assault of the Maoists on Liu Shao-
ch'i. Numerous articles in the official and unofficial press denouncing
the book and its author were published. In the mountains of diatribe
heaped upon Liu for producing this tract, several charges stand out. [132]
First, that it was intended to serve as a counterweight to the Thought
of Mao and to dilute its influence. Second, that by downgrading the
strength of contradictions in socialist society and emphasizing harmony,
the tract was designed to damp down the "class struggle" which Mao
was bent on sustaining. Third, that by putting the stress on "cen-

tralism" and hierarchical discipline rather than on "democracy," the
tract was meant to limit the initiative and to circumscribe the crea-
tivity of the basic-level Party members, as well as of the masses,
and to turn them into "docile tools" of the Party elite.

From the vantage point of hindsight, these charges appear to
be not without substance. In the face of Mao's growing pressure to
reverse the policies of retreat, the strategy of Party leaders opposing
Mao, as it seemed to be shaping up during this period, was not to
clash with the Chairman in a head-on confrontation, but to circumvent
his guidelines in the process of execution by subtle organizational
means. The implementation of such a strategy required that these
leaders maintain a firm hold over a tightly structured and responsive
Party organization. If so, then the republication and propagation of
Liu's article on "Self-Cultivation," with its emphasis on the subor-
dination of the Party members to the organization rather than to the
Chairman, and on inner-Party discipline, may have had a special
significance in the context of the simmering intraleadership conflict.
At any rate, the divergent organizational approaches between Mao and
Liu, as reflected in Liu's stand on the "reversal of verdicts" issue
and in his book on "Self-Cultivation," could not but have injected an
additional element of tension into the already strained relations between the two men and their supporters.

The Tenth Plenum

Given this build-up of tensions among the top leaders, it might
have been expected that the highly important Tenth Plenum, which
met at the end of the period of reappraisal in order to set down
long range policy guidelines, would be the scene of a clash between
Mao and leaders who opposed his views. As far as can be determined,
however, no such clash took place. And it did not take place because,
in line with the emerging pattern of leadership relations, when Mao
chose to exercise a policy-making initiative in Party councils, other
leaders did not press their views, but went along with the Chairman
insofar as the formulation of policy was concerned. As Liu said in
his "self-criticism": "It was only when the 10th Plenary Session in
September had adopted two resolutions and a communique that I cor-
rected my mistakes and the situation was basically altered."[133]

Mao took the initiative in a hard-hitting and self-confident speech
to the Plenum, in which he developed his thesis regarding the exis-

tence of contradictions in socialist society:

> . . . are there classes and class struggles in socialist
> countries? It can now be affirmed that there are definitely
> classes and class struggles in socialist countries. Lenin
> once said: After the victory of the revolution, because
> there is the bourgeoisie in the international arena, because
> there are still bourgeois remnants at home, and because
> the existence of the petty bourgeoisie will go on to give
> rise to the bourgeoisie, the overthrown classes will exist
> for a long time to come, and may even want to stage a
> comeback . . . For example, Yugoslavia has degenerated
> to become a revisionist country. [134]

Mao then emphasized that unless China combats this danger, it too
may become "revisionist":

> This country of ours must grasp well, know well and
> study well this question. We must acknowledge that
> classes and class struggles still exist for a long time
> to come, and that the reactionary classes may stage a
> comeback. We must heighten our vigilance and success-
> fully educate the young people, the cadres and the masses.
> The cadres at the intermediate and the grassroots levels
> must be educated, and the old cadres must also study
> and be educated. Otherwise, this country of ours will
> take the opposite course. [135]

Mao's thesis on "class struggle" was accepted by the Party
leaders, whatever may have been their true feelings. This was
indicated by the fact that the thesis was incorporated into the communique adopted by the Tenth Plenum:

> The Tenth Plenary Session of the Eighth Central Committee
> points out that throughout the historical period of proletarian
> revolution and proletarian dictatorship, throughout the his-
> torical period of transition from capitalism to communism
> (which will last scores of years or even longer), there is
> class struggle between the proletariat and the bourgeoisie
> and struggle between the socialist road and the capitalist
> road. The reactionary ruling classes which have been
> overthrown are not reconciled to their doom. They always
> attempt to stage a comeback. Meanwhile, there still exist

in society bourgeois influence, the force of habit of old
society and the spontaneous tendency towards capitalism
among part of the small producers. Therefore, among
the people, a small number of persons, making up only
a tiny fraction of the total population, who have not yet
undergone socialist remolding, always attempt to depart
from the socialist road and turn to the capitalist road
whenever there is an opportunity. Class struggle is
inevitable under these circumstances . . . We must
never forget it. [136]

Thus Mao issued his famous clarion-call: "Never forget class struggle. "

On balance, there can be little doubt that at the Tenth Plenum
Mao had his way. The political orientation of the Tenth Plenum
communique, with its emphasis on "class struggle" and its condem-
nation of "revisionism," was unmistakably Maoist. The economic
policies which emanated from the communique and the resolution on
the communes[137] were moderate, but, with their strong emphasis on
the preservation of the collective economy, were clearly acceptable
to Mao. It is not surprising, therefore, that in the Maoist interpretation of this period the Tenth Plenum is credited with having "stemmed
the evil wind for all-round restoration of capitalism whipped up by
Liu Shao-ch'i and others, defended the general line of the Party, the
Great Leap Forward and the people's commune, and defended Chairman
Mao and his proletarian revolutionary line. "[138]

Allowing for the exaggerations contained in this statement, at
first glance the Tenth Plenum does indeed appear as a major victory
for Mao. For it seemed to have put an end to the dissent and debates
which marked the period of reappraisal, and to have unified the Party
leadership behind Mao. Since there is substantial evidence to indicate that top Party leaders had disagreed with Mao up to the Plenum,
and continued to disagree thereafter, it is pertinent to ask how Mao
was able to have his views adopted without, as far as is known,
sparking a struggle within the leadership.

Part of the answer may lie in the assumption that dissenting
leaders decided to rally behind Mao due to the external pressures
impinging upon China at the time, namely, the threat of an invasion
from Taiwan and the Sino-Indian border conflict. [139] Such pressures,
however, could not have been more than a contributing factor, because

the Tenth Plenum was only one instance of Mao's ability to have his
views adopted in the highest Party councils despite the existence of
opposing opinions. In other instances during the period between the
Lushan Plenum and the Cultural Revolution, no outside threats existed
and yet Mao was still able to prevail over colleagues who were known
to hold different views.

The answer to Mao's political strength at a time of leadership
conflict must, therefore, be sought not in external factors but in the
internal workings and relationships of the ruling group. Since this
is one of the most obscure areas of Chinese politics, it is not possible to do more than to hypothesize, and here our hypothesis, already
alluded to, regarding the need to draw a distinction between the levels
of policy formulation and policy implementation seems to be highly
relevant. If this hypothesis is accepted, then it may be assumed
that Mao's ability to have the Party's decision-making bodies pass
resolutions in line with his desires despite the existence of opposing
views among the members of these bodies stemmed from two factors.
First, the tendency of top Party leaders to refrain from opposing
Mao forthrightly and openly in Party councils once the Chairman made
his wishes unequivocally clear. This tendency probably stemmed
from a combination of factors, including Mao's political power and
personal standing, his charismatic appeal and tactical skill, and
strains among the top leaders.[140] It was, however, not only Mao's
powers of manipulation that enabled him to get what appeared to be
his way at the Party conferences. For there was doubtless a second
factor in operation which, paradoxically, both greatly contributed to
his seeming success and detracted substantially from the thesis, favored by some analysts, that Mao was completely "in command" once
he decided to take personal charge of Party affairs at the Tenth Plenum and thereafter. This second factor derived from the firm hold
which high-level leaders had acquired over various sectors in the
huge Party organization. As the period between the Tenth Plenum
and the start of the Cultural Revolution would demonstrate, this hold
enabled them to reinterpret Mao's directives in the course of implementation according to their own views. For this reason they did
not have to oppose Mao directly, with all the risks and ramifications
that such a step would involve, but could achieve their objectives in
a much more subtle and safe manner. Put bluntly, leaders who
disagreed with Mao could afford to let the Chairman have the monopoly on words in the knowledge that they had the monopoly on the
levers of power.

In conclusion, it may be suggested that this dichotomy between policy formulation and policy implementation accounted in large part for Mao's seeming success at the Tenth Plenum. But in retrospect it appears that this very success contained within it the seeds of future failure. For if top leaders united behind Mao on the assumption that they would not have to carry out his directives, this unity was bound to disintegrate as the gap between Mao's desires and their deeds widened. The widening of this gap was, of course, the salient feature of Chinese politics from the Tenth Plenum until the Cultural Revolution. And it was Mao's determination to bridge this gap that finally drove him to assault the Party apparatus and its leaders.

The Tenth Plenum was thus a watershed between two periods. On the one hand, it signalled the end of the period of retreat and seemed to resolve the intraleadership differences which emerged at the Eighth Plenum, were suppressed during the period of retreat, and appeared again in a different form in the course of the policy reappraisal. In fact, however, the Tenth Plenum did not resolve these differences, but rather drove them beneath the surface, where they steadily heated up the political atmosphere until it reached a boiling point. The Tenth Plenum thus not only closed a chapter in leadership relations, but also marked the beginning of a new one-- the immediate prelude to the great struggle.

After the Tenth Plenum

Although the Maoist assertion that by the Tenth Plenum China had come to a "critical juncture" in the "violent struggle between the proletarian headquarters and the bourgeois headquarters"[141] is a gross exaggeration, there can be little doubt that in the months immediately preceding the Plenum the differences in policy approaches between Mao and other top Party leaders had crystallized to a point which seriously undermined leadership unity. In the aftermath of the Tenth Plenum these differences were played out mainly in the form of organizational conflicts, which broke into the open in the Cultural Revolution.

For some three years these conflicts escalated in the inner recesses of the Chinese power structure, but they were concealed by the placid surface of consensus and compromise, which had seemingly been reached at the Tenth Plenum. This divergence between the appearance of consensus and the reality of conflict stands out in

retrospect as the most striking feature of the Chinese political scene
in the period between the Tenth Plenum and the start of the Cultural
Revolution. The source of this divergence lay in the tactic employed
by many Party leaders to resist the implementation of Maoist directives. Instead of opposing Mao openly and head-on, they resorted to
the practice which Maoists term "waving red flags to oppose red
flags"; they feigned compliance by expressing commitment to Maoist
policies, but resisted in practice by deviating from these policies
in the process of implementation. As Mao increased his pressure,
the Party leaders increased their resistance, thereby widening the
gap between rhetoric and reality.

A reexamination of the post-Tenth Plenum period from the
perspective of hindsight and the revelations of the Cultural Revolution
lends credence to Maoist charges that the practice of "waving red
flags to oppose red flags" was, in fact, widespread in the Party
apparatus, especially at the highest levels. The most cogent illus-
tration of this tactic in operation was the Socialist Education Movement which, it is clear in retrospect, was characterized by intricate
maneuvering as Party leaders tried to damp down the revolutionary
fervor which Mao wanted to infuse into the Movement.[142] Whether
this tactic consisted of diluting, distorting, sidestepping, or sabotaging
Mao's directives, the result was the same: in his efforts to return
China to the revolutionary course which he had demanded at the Tenth
Plenum, Mao found himself increasingly balked and blocked by the
Party bureaucracy. In this way, policy differences became inextricably intertwined with power factors, setting the stage for a major
struggle among the top leaders.

By the beginning of 1965 Mao had apparently come to the conclusion that such a struggle was inevitable,[143] and by the summer
he was plainly contemplating the moves that would set it off. As
Mao remarked enigmatically to a foreign visitor: "I am alone with
the masses, waiting."[144] He did not wait long.

FOOTNOTES

1. For some discussions of intraleadership differences see Richard H. Solomon, Mao's Revolution and the Chinese Political Culture (Berkeley: 1971), pp. 268, passim; Parris H. Chang, "Struggle Between Two Roads in China's Countryside," Current Scene (Hong Kong), vol. VI, no. 3, February 15, 1968; John W. Lewis, "Leader, Commissar, and Bureaucrat: The Chinese Political System in the Last Days of the Revolution" and Comments by Michel Oksenberg; in Ping-ti Ho and Tang Tsou, ed., China in Crisis: China's Heritage and the Communist Political System, vol. 1, book 2 (Chicago: 1968), pp 449-500; Stuart R. Schram, "The Party in Chinese Communist Ideology;" in John W. Lewis, ed., Party Leadership and Revolutionary Power in China (Cambridge: 1970), pp. 170-202; Philip Bridgham, "Factionalism in the Central Committee," in Lewis, ed., Party Leadership, pp. 203-235; Ezra F. Vogel, Canton Under Communism: Programs and Politics in a Provincial Capital (Cambridge, Mass: 1969), p. 182, passim; Stuart R. Schram, "Mao Tse-tung and Liu Shao-ch'i, 1939-1969;" in Asian Survey, vol. XII, no. 4, April 1972, pp. 275-293; Stuart R. Schram, "The Cultural Revolution in Historical Perspective," in Schram, ed., Authority, Participation and Cultural Change in China (Cambridge University Press: 1973), pp. 1-108; Jack Gray, "The Two Roads: Alternative Strategies of Social Change and Economic Growth in China," in Schram, ed., Authority, pp. 109-157; Roderick MacFarquhar, The Origins of the Cultural Revolution: Contradictions Among the People (Oxford: 1974).

2. For some discussions of the significance of the Great Leap Forward see, for example, Franz Schurmann, Ideology and Organization in Communist China (Berkeley: 1966) esp. pp. 464-490; Stuart R. Schram, The Political Thought of Mao Tse-tung, revised and enlarged edition (New York: 1969), pp. 99-103; Vogel, ch. 6; Solomon, ch. XVIII.

3. See, for example, Benjamin Schwartz, "Modernization and the Maoist Vision--Some Reflections on Chinese Communist Goals"; in Roderick MacFarquhar, ed., China Under Mao: Politics Takes Command (Cambridge, Mass: 1966), pp. 3-19; Schurmann, Ideology and Organization, pp. 239-293; Franz Schurmann, "Economic Policy and Political Power in Communist China," in The Annals

59

of the American Academy of Political and Social Science, vol.
349, September 1963, pp. 49-64; Schram, Political Thought, pp.
80-98; Solomon, pp. 333-346, passim.

4. For a discussion of the differences between Soviet and Chinese
    motives for collectivization see Dwight Perkins, Market Control
    and Planning in Communist China (Cambridge, Mass: 1966),
    pp. 56-60. The problem of increasing the agricultural surplus
    while simultaneously raising rural living standards is dealt with
    in detail in David Ladd Denny, "Rural Policies and the Distri-
    bution of Agricultural Products in China, 1950-1959" (unpublished
    Ph. D. dissertation, University of Michigan, 1971).

5. Perkins, op. cit.; Denny, op. cit.; Schurmann, Ideology, pp.
    438-472.

6. Benjamin I. Schwartz, "China and the West in the 'Thought of
    Mao Tse-tung'," in China in Crisis, vol. 1, book 1, pp. 375-
    377, and "Modernization;" Stuart Schram, "Comments," in China
    in Crisis, vol. 1, book 1, pp. 384-86; Schurmann, Ideology and
    Organization, ch. IV: Schram, Political Thought, pp. 73-84;
    Solomon, pp. 333-346.

7. Schwartz, "China and the West," pp. 375-377; Schram, Political
    Thought, pp. 73-84.

8. See, for example, Schurmann, Ideology and Organization, pp.
    464-490; Vogel, ch. 6; Solomon, ch. XVIII.

9. In this connection see Maurice Meisner, "Leninism and Maoism:
    Some Populist Perspectives on Marxism-Leninism in China," in
    The China Quarterly, no. 45, January-March 1971, pp. 2-36.

10. This, of course, does not imply that the Great Leap was not
    preceded by vigorous debates, nor that there were no dissenters
    among the top leaders. What it does imply is that once the
    leadership started moving in the direction of the Great Leap,
    most of the top leaders rallied behind Mao, at least during the
    initial stages of the Great Leap, and while leaders such as Ch'en
    Yun, who clearly opposed this venture, were apparently shunted
    aside, there is no substantial evidence of the type of subtle re-
    sistance that was to characterize the attitude of many top leaders
    toward Maoist policies in the first half of the 1960s.

11.   See, for example, Vogel, ch. 6 and Solomon, ch. XVIII.

12.   Vogel, ch. 6.

13.   This is still a moot point, with respect to which Stuart Schram's observations are particularly relevant. In Schram's view, the replacement of Mao by Liu as Chairman of the Republic:

> . . . was not, as some people thought at the time, the consequence of the blow to Mao's prestige which resulted from the difficulties encountered by his economic policies, for it had been made known within the Party at the end of 1957, and inscribed in the "Sixty Articles on Work Methods" in January 1958 . . . It is possible, however, that Mao nevertheless felt humiliated by the fact that his retirement took place at a time when his policies had not been conspicously successful, and that others in the Party may have been glad to see him go. This may well have been the case even though Liu, who had been identified with the Great Leap, appeared to some extent as a symbol of continuity, in comparison with other possible candidates for the post of head of state.

Stuart R. Schram, "Mao Tse-tung and Liu Shao-ch'i," pp. 287-288.

14.   See, for example, Vogel, pp. 259-262; Solomon, pp. 368-373.

15.   Accounts of the P'eng Teh-huai Affair can be found in: David A. Charles, "The Dismissal of Marshal P'eng Teh-huai," in The China Quarterly, no. 8, October-December 1961, pp. 63-76; J. D. Simmonds, "P'eng Teh-huai: A Chronological Re-examination," in The China Quarterly, no. 37, January-March 1969, pp. 120-138; Frederick C. Teiwes, "A Review Article: The Evolution of Leadership Purges in Communist China," in The China Quarterly, no. 41, January-March 1970, pp. 121-134; Philip Bridgham, "Factionalism in the Central Committee," in Lewis, Party Leadership, pp. 203-235.   For documentary collections see The Case of P'eng Teh-huai 1959-1968 (Hong Kong: Union Research Institute, 1969), and "The Wicked History

of P'eng Teh-huai," a pamphlet compiled in November 1967 by Tsinghua University's Chingkang Mountain Corps under the Capital Red Guard Congress, in CB, no. 851, April 26, 1968.

16. "Wicked History," pp. 19-23.

17. Ibid., p. 18.

18. Ibid., p. 19.

19. Ibid., p. 20.

20. Ibid., p. 25.

21. Ibid., p. 20.

22. Ibid., p. 21.

23. Ibid.

24. Ibid., p. 22.

25. Ibid.

26. Ibid., p. 19, and p. 22.

27. Ibid., p. 22.

28. Ibid., p. 20.

29. Cf. note 13.

30. "Wicked History," p. 18. During his interrogation P'eng said that the difficulties which he foresaw had moved him to compose a poem:

> Grain is scattered on the ground and the potato
> plants have withered. The young and able-bodied
> persons have gone to smelt iron, and young boys
> and girls are left to attend to farm work.
> How are they going to be fed next year?
> Please think of the people.

31. That the morale of the troops plummeted as a result of the agricultural crisis has been extensively documented by the secret army publication Kung-tso Tung-hsun [Bulletin of activities]. For a translation, see J. Chester Cheng, ed., The Politics of the Chinese Red Army (The Hoover Institution, Stanford University: 1966).

32. See Ellis Joffe, Party and Army: Professionalism and Political Control in the Chinese Officer Corps, 1949-1964 (Harvard University: East Asian Research Center, 1965), pp. 84-86.

33. Joffe, pp. 91-101; see also John Gittings, The Role of the Chinese Army (Oxford: 1967), pp. 235-241; and Alice Langley Hsieh, Communist China's Military Policies, Doctrine, and Strategy: A Lecture Presented at the National Defense College Tokyo, September 17, 1968 (The RAND Corporation: October 1968), pp. 15-17.

34. See Joffe, Gittings, and Hsieh in note 33. See also Mao's "Speech at the Symposium of Group Leaders of the Enlarged Meeting of the Military Commission (Excerpts)," in Mao chu-hsi tui P'eng, Huang, Chang, Chou fan-tang chi-t'uan ti p'i-pan [Chairman Mao's criticism and repudiation of the P'eng, Huang, Chang, and Chou anti-Party clique]. This is a Red Guard pamphlet that has no publisher and no date. It has been translated in Chinese Law and Government, vol. 1, no. 4, Winter 1968-69, and also by the American Consulate-General, Hong Kong, in SCMM-Supplement, no. 21, April 2, 1968. Page citations are to the SCMM-S. Mao's above-mentioned speech is on pp. 5-8.

35. For a discussion of the strategic issues see Joffe, Gittings, and Hsieh in note 33.

36. Donald S. Zagoria, The Sino-Soviet Conflict, 1956-1961 (Princeton: 1962), pp. 77-141.

37. It is possible that the Soviets hinted to P'eng in some way that they might reinstate the nuclear aid agreement which they had abrogated in June 1959. It is not inconceivable, moreover, that one reason for Khrushchev's abrogation of the agreement was to show the Chinese that he was no "paper tiger," and in this way to bring pressure upon them. If so, Khrushchev, like P'eng,

grossly misread the mood of the Chinese leadership, for the cancellation of the agreement apparently only strengthened their determination not to give in to Soviet pressures, but rather to strive for "self-reliance." P'eng's preference for reliance on the Soviets instead of "self-reliance" may explain the charge levelled at him during the Cultural Revolution to the effect that:

> He opposed the policy advanced by Chairman Mao of creating an independent and complete network of modern national defense industried by relying on our own efforts . . . He depended entirely on the Khrushchev revisionist clique for the improvement of our army's equipment and the development of up-to-date military science and technology.

"Settle Accounts with P'eng Teh-huai for his Heinous Crimes of Usurping Army Leadership and Opposing the Party," People's Daily, August 20, 1967; Peking NCNA International Service in English, August 20, 1967.

38. If P'eng indeed made such an argument, it would presumably be in order to appeal to colleagues whose primary concern was economic development rather than China's strategic posture.

39. Cf. Charles, "Dismissal."

40. "Wicked History," p. 14.

41. "Principal Crimes of P'eng Teh-huai, Big Ambitionist and Schemer," Chingkang Mountains and Kwangtung Literary and Art Combat Bulletin; Canton, September 5, 1967; in The Case of P'eng, p. 180.

42. Excerpts from the "Resolution Concerning the Anti-Party Clique Headed by P'eng Teh-huai," adopted on August 16, 1959 at the Eighth Plenary Session of the Eighth Central Committee; Peking NCNA International Service in English, August 15, 1967.

43. "Speech Delivered by Mao Tse-tung at the Enlarged Meeting of the Military Commission of the CCP Central Committee and the Conference on Foreign Affairs" (September 11, 1959); in "Chairman Mao's Criticism," p. 37.

44. This, of course, is evident from the whole subsequent course of leadership relations. For one contemporary indication that many leaders agreed with P'eng's views of the Great Leap, see Mao's speech of July 23, 1959 at Lushan, in The Case of P'eng, pp. 15-26 and in "Chairman Mao's Criticism," pp. 11-18.

45. Purged along with P'eng and named in Red Guard documents were Huang K'o-ch'eng, PLA chief-of-staff and secretary of the Central Committee, Chang Wen-t'ien, vice-minister of foreign affairs and alternate member of the Politburo, and Chou Hsiao-chou, first secretary of the Hunan Party committee and alternate member of the Politburo. There is no doubt that these men openly supported P'eng at Lushan. However, what they said is not known. Nor have the Chinese revealed the identity of the other members of the clique at Lushan, although it is possible to infer who some of them were. See Bridgham, pp. 215-216.

46. Schurmann, Ideology and Organization, pp. 45-46.

47. "Selected Edition on Liu Shao-ch'i's Counterrevolutionary Revisionist Crimes," pamphlet published by the Liaison Station "Pledging to Fight a Bloody Battle with Liu-Teng-T'ao to the End," attached to August 18 Red Rebel Regiment of Nank'ai University, April 1967; in SCMM, no. 652, April 28, 1969, p. 30.

48. See note 43.

49. The Case of P'eng, p. 25. See also Teiwes, p. 128.

50. "Chairman Mao's Criticism," p. 14.

51. "Resolution."

52. See, for example, the articles reproduced in The Case of P'eng, part III.

53. Note 42, p. 39. This also became apparent when the question of "reversal of verdicts" became an issue in the intraleadership conflict. See pp. 50-52 below.

54. Liu Lan-tao, "The Chinese Communist Party is the Supreme Commander of the Chinese People in Building Socialism," People's Daily, September 28, 1959; in The Case of P'eng, p. 106.

55. Solomon, pp. 395-400. It is noteworthy that among the top leaders only Lin Piao wrote a review praising the Fourth Volume.

56. See, for example, John W. Lewis, "China's Secret Military Papers: Continuities and Revelations," in China Under Mao, pp. 63-67; and Franz Schurmann, "Peking's Recognition of Crisis," in Albert Feuerwerker, ed., Modern China (New Jersey: 1965), p. 89, passim.

57. See, for example, Vogel, pp. 269, 279, 296-297.

58. See, for example, Choh-ming Li, "China's Industrial Development, 1956-1963," in China Under Mao, pp. 199-201; Vogel, pp. 271-296; Schurmann, "Peking's Recognition."

59. See, for example, "Thirty-Three Leading Counterrevolutionary Revisionists," a Red Guard pamphlet for which no details are given; in CB, no. 874, March 17, 1969, p. 6.

60. Cf. Maurice Meisner, "Maoist Utopianism and the Future of Chinese Society," in International Journal (Canadian Institute of International Affairs), vol. XXVI, Summer 1971, pp. 535-555; see also by Meisner "Utopian Goals and Ascetic Values in Chinese Communist Ideology," in Journal of Asian Studies, vol. 28, no. 1, November 1968, pp. 101-110, and "Leninism and Maoism"; Schwartz, "Modernization"; Schram, Political Thought, pp. 15-144.

61. "Chairman Mao's Criticism," p. 12-13.

62. Ibid., p. 39.

63. For a psychohistorical interpretation see Robert J. Lifton, Revolutionary Immortality: Mao Tse-tung and the Chinese Cultural Revolution (New York: 1968).

64. Along the Socialist or the Captialist Road? (Peking: Foreign Languages Press, 1968), pp. 36-37.

65. For a discussion of this complex question see MacFarquhar, Origins, pp. 152-156.

66. "Outline of the Struggle Between the Two Lines from the Eve of the Founding of the People's Republic of China Through the 11th Plenum of the 8th CCP Central Committee." This is a pamphlet the text of which was reproduced from the Shanghai Chieh-fang Jih-pao; in CB, no. 884, July 18, 1969, p. 18.

67. Cf. Solomon, pp. 405-431.

68. Cf. Merle Goldman, "Party Policies Toward the Intellectuals: The Unique Blooming and Contending of 1961-1962," in Lewis, Party Leadership, pp. 291-292.

69. Yao Wen-yuan, "On 'Three-Family Village'--The Reactionary Nature of 'Evening Chats at Yenshan' and 'Notes from Three-Family Village'"; originally published in Shanghai's Chieh-fang Jih-pao and Wen-hui pao on May 10, 1966; in The Great Socialist Cultural Revolution in China (1) (Peking: Foreign Languages Press, 1966), p. 34.

70. "From the Defeat of P'eng Teh-huai to the Bankruptcy of China's Khrushchev," Hung-ch'i [Red flag], no. 13, 1967; in The Case of P'eng, p. 138.

71. Yao Wen-yuan, p. 31, and Kao Chu, "Open Fire at the Black Anti-Party and Anti-Socialist Line"; originally published in the Liberation Army Daily, May 8, 1966; in The Great Socialist Cultural Revolution in China (2) (Peking: Foreign Languages Press, 1966), p. 3.

72. Kao Chu, p. 3, and "Teng To's Evening Chats at Yenshan is Anti-Party and Anti-Socialist Double-Talk"; originally published in the Liberation Army Daily and the Kuangming Daily, May 8, 1966; The Great (2), p. 20.

73. "Teng To's," pp. 13-14.

74. Ibid., pp. 24-25.

75. Ibid., pp. 15-18 and 24.

68

76. Ibid., p. 39.

77. Donald Klein and Anne Clark, Biographic Dictionary of Chinese Communism, 1921-1965 (Cambridge, Mass: 1971), pp. 713-718.

78. That P'eng felt, and was held, responsible for the actions of the Peking writers was indicated by his risky effort to block Mao's campaign against them in the winter of 1965-1966, an effort that was presumably prompted first and foremost by his desire to protect himself.

79. "Before and After the 'Grandview House' Counterrevolutionary Incident," in "Counterrevolutionary Revisionist P'eng Chen's Towering Crimes of Opposing the Party, Socialism and the Thought of Mao Tse-tung"; published by the Liaison Center for Thorough Criticism of Liu-Teng-T'ao, Tungfanghung Commune, China University of Science and Technology, Red Guard Congress; in SCMM, no. 640, January 13, 1969, p. 19.

80. Ibid., pp. 19-21.

81. Ibid., p. 22.

82. Ibid., p. 23.

83. Ibid., pp. 25-27.

84. Ibid., p. 30.

85. This charge appears to be trumped up primarily because there is no evidence that Liu and Teng had planned to make, or had made, a "surprise attack" at the January conference. The forthright comments which they, and especially Liu, made at the conference must be seen in the context of the policy reappraisal that was going on among the leaders at that time. Nor is there any indication that at that conference they had "lost the battle." For details see the discussion of the January conference, pp. 40-45.

86. "Chiang Ch'ing's Speech at the Enlarged Meeting of the Military Commission of the CCP Central Committee on April 12, 1967; in Issues and Studies (Taipei), July, 1970, p. 83.

87. "Chairman Mao's Criticism," p. 42.

88. The major decisions adopted by the Central Committee at critical junctures during this period, namely the Lushan Resolution and the Tenth Plenum Connunique, clearly indicate that Mao was "in command" at this level of policy-making.

89. One of the strangest, and yet strongest, indications lies in the discrepancies between the remarks attributed to Liu in the Red Guard pamphlets and the interpretations given these remarks by the Red Guards. Almost invariably the interpretations attributed extreme intentions to the remarks which are simply not borne out by the remarks themselves, suggesting that, though given out of context, the remarks are genuine. In order to build their case against Liu, the Red Guards were forced to make accusations which are not substantiated by Liu's comments which they themselves reproduced.

90. "Selected Edition," p. 25.

91. Cf. Schram, "Mao Tse-tung and Liu Shao-ch'i," p. 286.

92. "Selected Edition," p. 25.

93. Ibid.

94. "Record of Teng Hsiao-p'ing's Reactionary Utterances"; a pamphlet published by the Liaison Post for Criticizing Liu, Teng, and T'ao, "Red Flag" Commune of the Peking Railways Institute, Red Guard Congress, April 1967; in SCMP-Supplement, no. 208, October 26, 1967, p. 13.

95. "Selected Edition," p. 24.

96. Ibid., pp. 24 and 22.

97. Ibid., p. 27.

98. Ibid., p. 22.

99. Ibid., p. 24.

100. Ibid., p. 5.

101. Ibid., p. 22.

102. "Record," p. 11.

103. "Down with the Old Swine Chu Teh," Peking Tung-fang-hung [The East is red], February 11, 1967; in SCMP-Supplement, no. 172, p. 23.

104. "Outline of the Struggle," p. 19.

105. "Talks and Writings of Chairman Mao"; articles from an untitled and undated pamphlet; in Translations on Communist China, no. 128, JPRS 52029, December 21, 1970, pp. 1-18.

106. Cf. Schram, "Mao Tse-tung and Liu Shao-ch'i," pp. 289-290.

107. "Talks and Writings," p. 12.

108. Ibid., p. 9.

109. See, for example, The Struggle Between the Two Roads in China's Countryside, by the editorial departments of Jen-min Jih-pao, Hung ch'i and Chieh-fang Chün-pao, November 23, 1967 (Peking: Foreign Languages Press, 1968), pp. 15-17.

110. This was evident from numerous refugee reports. See also collection of documents in Union Research Service (Hong Kong: Union Research Institute), vol. XXVII, nos. 7-9, April 24, April 27, and May 1, 1962.

111. The Struggle, p. 15.

112. "Selected Edition," p. 23.

113. "Thirty-Three Leading," p. 11.

114. "Selected Edition," p. 23.

115. Ibid., p. 26.

116. "Outline of the Struggle," p. 20.

117. Parris H. Chang, "Research Notes on the Changing Loci of the Decision in the CCP," The China Quarterly, no. 44, October-December 1970, p. 191.

118. "Talks and Writings," p. 19-20.

119. Ibid., p. 20.

120. Ibid., pp. 22-27.

121. "Selected Edition," p. 23.

122. "Principal Crimes of P'eng Teh-huai," p. 178-179, and "The Criminal History of Big Conspirator, Big Ambitionist, Big Warlord P'eng Teh-huai"; this is a document taken from the "Collected Materials on P'eng Teh-huai," published in late 1967 by the Peking Red Guard Congress, Tsinghua University, Chingkanshan Corps; in The Case of P'eng, pp. 206-207.

123. See, for example, "Outline of the Struggle," p. 19.

124. Ibid.

125. See note 46.

126. "Selected Edition," p. 30.

127. Ibid., p. 28.

128. Cf. Schram, "Mao Tse-tung and Liu Shao-ch'i," p. 285; Schurmann, Ideology and Organization, pp. 514-519; John Wilson Lewis, "Leader, Commissar, and Bureaucrat: The Chinese Political System in the Last Days of the Revolution," China in Crisis, pp. 455-457.

129. "Selected Edition," pp. 28-29.

130. "Selected Edition on Liu Shao-ch'i's Counterrevolutionary Revisionist Crimes"; in SCMM, no. 651, April 22, 1969, p. 39.

131. "Chairman Mao's Criticism," pp. 40, 41.

132. See, for example, "Betrayal of Proletarian Dictatorship is the Heart of the Book on 'Self-Cultivation'" by the editorial departments of Hung-ch'i and Jen-min Jih-pao, May 8, 1967; "Bury the Slave Mentality Advocated by the Khrushchev of China,"

People's Daily, April 6, 1967; Peking NCNA Domestic Service, April 6, 1967; and "Thoroughly Eradicate the Big Poisonous Weed 'Self-Cultivation'," article broadcast by Peking Domestic Service, April 5, 1967.

133. "Selected Edition," SCMM, no. 652, p. 23.

134. "Chairman Mao's Criticism," p. 38.

135. Ibid.

136. The Case of P'eng, p. 334.

137. Documents of the Chinese Communist Party Central Committee: September 1956-April 1969, vol. 1 (Hong Kong: Union Research Institute, 1971), pp. 185-192 and 193-205.

138. "Outline of the Struggle," p. 20.

139. See, for example, Allen S. Whiting, "The Use of Force in Foreign Policy by the People's Republic of China," The Annals of the American Academy of Political and Social Science, vol. 402, July 1972, p. 58.

140. It need hardly be emphasized again that the state of leadership relations throughout the post-1959 period remains a highly obscure question.   Nonetheless, it may be assumed with considerable certainty that the leaders who came to comprise the Opposition to Mao and his policies did not constitute a monolithic body.   It may be further assumed that Mao was aware of this and that he used the strains among his colleagues against them.

141. "Outline of the Struggle," p. 20.

142. For a summary and documentation, see Stuart R. Schram, "The Cultural Revolution in Historical Perspective," in Stuart R. Schram, ed., Authority, Participation and Cultural Change in China (Cambridge University Press: 1973), pp. 73-85.

143. Ibid., pp. 84-85.

144. Andre Malraux, Anti-Memoirs (New York: 1968), p. 375. quoted in Solomon, p. 452.

MICHIGAN PAPERS IN CHINESE STUDIES

No. 1. The Chinese Economy, 1912-1949, by Albert Feuerwerker.

No. 2. The Cultural Revolution: 1967 in Review, four essays by Michel Oksenberg, Carl Riskin, Robert Scalapino, and Ezra Vogel.

No. 3. Two Studies in Chinese Literature. "One Aspect of Form in the Arias of Yüan Opera" by Dale Johnson; and "Hsü K'o's Huang Shan Travel Diaries" translated by Li Chi, with an introduction, commentary, notes, and bibliography by Chun-shu Chang.

No. 4. Early Communist China: Two Studies. "The Fu-t'ien Incident" by Ronald Suleski; and "Agrarian Reform in Kwangtung, 1950-1953" by Daniel Bays.

No. 5. The Chinese Economy, ca. 1870-1911, by Albert Feuerwerker.

No. 6. Chinese Paintings in Chinese Publications, 1956-1968: An Annotated Bibliography and An Index to the Paintings, by E. J. Laing.

No. 7. The Treaty Ports and China's Modernization: What Went Wrong? by Rhoads Murphey.

No. 8. Two Twelfth Century Texts on Chinese Painting, "Shan-shui ch'un-ch'üan chi" by Han Cho, and chapters nine and ten of "Hua-chi" by Teng Ch'un, translated by Robert J. Maeda.

No. 9. The Economy of Communist China, 1949-1969, by Chu-yuan Cheng.

No. 10. Educated Youth and the Cultural Revolution in China, by Martin Singer.

No. 11. Premodern China: A Bibliographic Introduction, by Chun-shu Chang.

No. 12. Two Studies on Ming History, by Charles O. Hucker.

No. 13. Nineteenth Century China: Five Imperialist Perspectives, selected by Dilip Basu, edited with an introduction by Rhoads Murphey.

No. 14. Modern China, 1840-1972: An Introduction to Sources and Research Aids, by Andrew J. Nathan.

No. 15. Women in China: Studies in Social Change and Feminism, edited with an introduction by Marilyn B. Young.

No. 16. An Annotated Bibliography of Chinese Painting Catalogues and Related Texts, by Hin-cheung Lovell.

No. 17. China's Allocation of Fixed Capital Investment, 1952-57, by Chu-yuan Cheng.

No. 18. Health, Conflict, and the Chinese Political System, by David M. Lampton.

No. 19. Chinese and Japanese Music-Dramas, edited by J. I. Crump and William P. Malm.

No. 20. Hsin-lun (New Treatise) and Other Writings by Huan T'an (43 B.C.-28 A.D.), translated by Timoteus Pokora.

No. 21. Rebellion in Nineteenth-Century China, by Albert Feuerwerker.

No. 22. Between Two Plenums: China's Intraleadership Conflict, 1959-1962, by Ellis Joffe.

Price: $3.00 (US) each
except $4.00 for special issues #6, #15, and #19
and $5.00 for #20

Prepaid Orders Only

NONSERIES PUBLICATION

Index to the "Chan-Kuo Ts'e", by Sharon Fidler and J. I. Crump. A companion volume to the Chan Kuo Ts'e translated by J. I. Crump. (Oxford: Clarendon Press, 1970). $3.00

MICHIGAN ABSTRACTS OF CHINESE AND
JAPANESE WORKS ON CHINESE HISTORY

No. 1. The Ming Tribute Grain System by Hoshi Ayao, translated
by Mark Elvin.

No. 2. Commerce and Society in Sung China by Shiba Yoshinobu,
translated by Mark Elvin.

No. 3. Transport in Transition: The Evolution of Traditional
Shipping in China, translations by Andrew Watson.

No. 4. Japanese Perspectives on China's Early Modernization: The
Self-Strengthening Movement, 1860-1895, by K. H. Kim.

Price: $4.00 (US) each

Prepaid Orders Only

Michigan Papers and Abstracts available from:
Center for Chinese Studies
University of Michigan
Lane Hall
Ann Arbor, Michigan 48104
USA

Printed and bound by CPI Group (UK) Ltd, Croydon, CR0 4YY